MEDWAY

MEDWAY

VIRGINIA CHRISTIAN BEACH

Virginia Christian Beach

PRINCIPAL PHOTOGRAPHY BY
THOMAS BLAGDEN, JR.

WYRICK & COMPANY

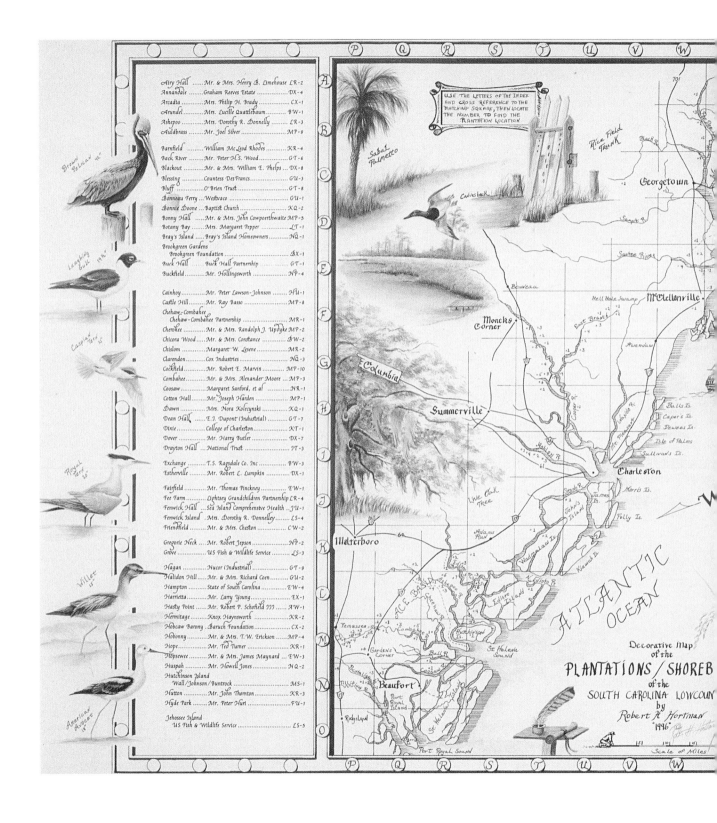

Airy Hall ....Mr. & Mrs. Henry B. Limehouse ..LR-2
Annandale ....Graham Reeves Estate DX-4
Arcadia ....Mrs. Philip H. Brady CX-1
Arundel ....Mrs. Lucille Quattlebaum BW-1
Ashepoo ....Mrs. Dorothy R. Donnelly LR-3
Auldbrass ....Mr. Joel Silver MP-9

Barnfield ....William Mc Leod Rhodes KR-4
Back River ......Mr. Peter H.S. Wood GT-6
Blackout ....Mr. & Mrs. William E. Phelps DX-8
Blessing ....Countess Des Francs GU-3
Bluff ....O'Brien Trust GT-8
Bonneau Ferry ...Westvaco GU-1
Bonnie Doone ....Baptist Church KQ-2
Bonny Hall ......Mr. & Mrs. John Cowporthwaite MP-5
Botany Bay ......Mrs. Margaret Pepper LT-1
Bray's Island ...Bray's Island Homeowners NQ-1
Brookgreen Gardens
  Brookgreen Foundation BX-1
Buck Hall ....Buck Hall Partnership GT-1
Buckfield ....Mr. Hollingsworth NP-4

Cainhoy ....Mr. Peter Lawson-Johnson HU-1
Castle Hill .....Mr. Ray Basso MP-8
Chehaw-Combahee
  Chehaw-Combahee Partnership MR-1
Cherokee ....Mr. & Mrs. Randolph J. Updyke MP-2
Chicora Wood ....Mr. & Mrs. Constance BW-2
Chislom ....Margaret W. Lesene MR-2
Clarendon ....Cox Industries NQ-3
Cockfield ....Mr. Robert E. Marvin MP-10
Combahee ....Mr. & Mrs. Alexander Moore MP-3
Coosaw ....Margaret Sanford, et al NR-1
Cotton Hall .....Mr. Joseph Harden MP-1
Dawn ....Mrs. Nora Kolecynski KQ-1
Dean Hall .......E.I. Dupont (Industrial) GT-7
Dixie ....College of Charleston KT-1
Dover ....Mr. Harry Butler DX-7
Drayton Hall ....National Trust IT-3

Exchange ........T.S. Ragsdale Co. Inc BW-3
Estherville .....Mr. Robert L. Lumpkin DX-1

Fairfield ....Mr. Thomas Pinckney EW-1
Fee Farm ....Lightsey Grandchildren Partnership .LR-4
Fenwick Hall ....Sea Island Comprehensive Health ...JU-1
Fenwick Island ..Mrs. Dorothy R. Donnelley LS-4
Friendfield .....Mr. & Mrs. Cheston CW-2

Gregorie Neck ...Mr. Robert Jepson NP-2
Grove ....US Fish & Wildlife Service LS-3

Hagan ....Nucor (Industrial) GT-9
Haldon Hill .....Mr. & Mrs. Richard Coen GU-2
Hampton ....State of South Carolina EW-4
Harrietta ....Mr. Larry Young EX-1
Hasty Point .....Mr. Robert P. Schofield III AW-1
Hermitage ....Knox Haynsworth KR-2
Hobcaw Barony ...Baruch Foundation CX-2
Hobonny ....Mr. & Mrs. T.W. Erickson MP-4
Hope ....Mr. Ted Turner MP-6
Hopsewee ....Mr. & Mrs. James Maynard EW-3
Huspah ....Mr. Howell Jones NQ-2
Hutchinson Island
  Wall/Johnson/Buntrock MS-1
Hutton ....Mr. John Thornton KR-3
Hyde Park ....Mr. Peter Hurt FU-1

Jehossee Island
  US Fish & Wildlife Service LS-5

USE THE LETTERS OF THE INDEX AND CROSS REFERENCE TO THE MATCHING SQUARE, THEN LOCATE THE NUMBER TO FIND THE PLANTATION LOCATION

Sabal Palmetto
Canvasback
Rice Field Trunk

Georgetown
Black R.
Sampit R.
Santee River

Bonneau
Hell Hole Swamp
McClellanville
East Branch
Awendaw

Moncks Corner
Columbia
Summerville

Cooper R.
Bulls Is.
Caper's Is.
Dewees Is.
Isle of Palms
Mt. Pleasant
Sullivan's Is.

Charleston
Morris Is.
James Is.
John's Island
Folly Is.

Live Oak Tree
Adams Run
Waterboro
Wadmalaw Is.
Kiawah R.
Edisto R.
Edisto Island

ATLANTIC OCEAN

ACE BASIN
Ashepoo R.
Combahee R.
Temassee
Hutchinson Is.
Bull R.
St. Helena Sound

Gardens Corner
Pocotaligo
Beaufort
Coosaw R.
St. Helena Island

Ridgeland
Port Royal Island

Port Royal Sound

Decorative Map of the PLANTATIONS / SHOREB of the SOUTH CAROLINA LOWCOUN by Robert A. Hortman 1996

Scale of Miles

CONTENTS

FOREWORD

I have lived under the magic of Medway for 70 years. The strong silent oaks with their branches of dripping moss cast their spell of mystery.

The lyrics of songbirds and the fragrance of sweet olive bushes fill the spring air. The scent of wisteria and jasmine float on the warm evening. I hear an owl hoot and the melody of a whippoorwill.

Long shadows stretch across the lawn, and darkness falls gently, enveloping everything in tranquillity and silence.

In the words of Hervey Allen:

Here restless Time himself has come to rest.

I saw him once asleep
Down by the dark ponds
Where alligators creep.
He had been fishing with a willow withe,
And by him lay his hourglass and scythe,
Resting upon the grass;
They lay there in the sun,
And through the glass the sands had ceased to run.

The peace of Medway permeates my soul.

Gertrude Sanford Legendre

INTRODUCTION
by
Virginia Christian Beach

I first saw Medway on a cold night in December of 1989. My husband and I sped down the long, dirt drive, then slowed as it dipped slightly and carried us across a causeway. We looked ahead through silhouettes of dense, moss-draped live oaks and saw an enormous ball of orange-yellow light. As we approached, a tall house emerged out of the trees and its gabled roof climbed like a stairway to the rising moon.

We walked to the river entrance and knocked. Sam Washington, Medway's chief houseman, ushered us out of the darkness into a bright hall. We entered an adjacent room and found a dozen or so guests engaged in conversation. The small, square compartment was encased from floor to ceiling with old cypress paneling and lined with books, guns and exotic souvenirs from distant lands. A middle eastern carpet covered the floor, and armchairs and footstools were pulled close to the fire.

Our hostess, Gertrude Sanford Legendre, greeted us with her characteristic "So nice to see you!" and introduced us around. Among the guests were Russell Train, president of World Wildlife Fund and former EPA chief under Gerald Ford, and Peter Manigault, publisher of the Charleston Post and Courier and descendant of rice planters. Wildlife artist and photographer John Henry Dick, son of the widow of John Jacob Astor, sat next to Gertrude. Bill Baldwin, preeminent South Carolina wildlife biologist and forester, and his wife, Agnes, a local historian, were also present, along with Bob Hortman, the plantation manager.

The ethereal loveliness of the plantation permeated the evening. Gathered for the purpose of discussing conservation, we were, in a sense, carrying on Medway's 300-year attachment of people to the land. From the strength and constancy of the land, people have derived the resources to fight the forces of change, decay and loss. The old brick house, made from the soil and reaching for the moon, was more than just a romantic image; it was a tangible link between the land and human aspirations.

Indeed, the house at Medway is the centerpiece of the plantation, and its site is one of the longest continually occupied properties in the Lowcountry. Built in 1704 or 1705, it is the oldest masonry structure standing in South Carolina today. Historians suspect that the house may be built on the foundations of the original 1692 structure that burned. On the surrounding grounds lies possibly the oldest marked grave (1694) in the state and perhaps the only remaining marked grave of a proprietary governor in South Carolina.

The plantation lands consist of 6,728 acres of native longleaf pine forests, rich bottomland swamps, meandering tidal wetlands, remnant rice fields and luxuriant gardens. Bounded by the upper reaches of Back River, a tributary of the historic Cooper River that flows into Charleston Harbor, this National Register plantation remains much as it was three centuries ago.

English and Dutch colonists first claimed Medway in 1685 and 1686, respectively. At that time, physical geography mattered. Everyone lived relatively close to the land. (Weir, 1983) Whether hunting for meat or skins, felling timber, driving livestock or tilling the soil, the Etiwan Indians, Europeans and African slaves, in one way or another, relied on the land for their survival.

The Europeans viewed the natural world as a source of personal wealth; hence their desire to own land. The land would, in turn, fuel their aspirations for nobility. They believed that through the domination and ordering of the landscape, they could attain not only wealth but also a standing in society akin to the Old World landed aristocracies.

Originally, as historian Robert Stockton writes, "Berkeley County [where Medway is located] was the home of small agrarian and hunting tribes of Native Americans. They included the Etiwan or Eutaw, a tribe of the Muscogean linguistic group, who occupied the vicinity of the Cooper River, which at one time was called the Etiwan River."

As these Indians were driven from their ancestral lands and decimated by slavery, disease and war, the African slaves and their progeny became new permanent residents. Their bondage and its hardships, combined with their West African traditions, would engender yet another distinct, powerful relationship to the land. Unlike "absentee planters or transient overseers," slaves were often recognized as knowing the plantations better than their owners. (Chaplin, 1992) The land infused every aspect of slave society. Later generations of Medway residents would continue farming and hunting, but not necessarily as their primary livelihood. By the end of the 19th century and into the 20th, Medway, like so many Lowcountry plantations, evolved into a hunting retreat. The old pine and rice lands became reserves prized for their wild game. The Stoney family, who owned Medway for almost one hundred years, and the Gourdine family, who served them, were renowned for their hunting prowess, storytelling and knowledge of the land.

Gertrude and Sidney Legendre bought Medway from the Stoneys in 1929. The young couple were part of a northern migration south, financier and industrialist families for the most part, in search of good quail and duck shooting and a retreat from the pace of life in the urban northeast. The transfer from Stoney to Legendre (from southern to northern hands) and, subsequently, Gertrude Legendre's long tenure at Medway tell a modern story of evolving land values that culminates in her 1991 donation of permanent conservation easements on the plantation–the ultimate act of stability in a century of precipitous change.

The most remarkable aspect of Medway's story is that the plantation survives. "Tragical" and "ancient" (to quote novelist John Bennett's 1906 description), Medway was nearly lost more than once. Expanded, shrunken, then expanded again, portions were sold off for taxes, used as collateral, traded and finally reclaimed. Medway withstood the Revolutionary War and the Civil War. Hurricanes and earthquakes shook the house and wrecked the gardens, yet the plantation remained. Now acid rain and urban sprawl pose new threats.

This book aims to capture both the constancy and the transforming power of Medway. So many forces have pulled against it–economic adversity, natural disasters, war, the poverty of a region, greed– yet Medway endures and continues to inspire. It is an anchor for a vibrant society of family, friends, artists, visitors and workers. From resident craftsmen to visiting statesmen and philanthropists, to lords and ladies from abroad, Medway magnetizes all who know it. Here is a place where nature, art, society and work can thrive in near perfect balance.

Photographer Tom Blagden, a family friend of Gertrude's, is one such artist who has been deeply inspired by the plantation. He moved to the Lowcountry early in his career and developed a close friendship with artist John Henry Dick. It was with John Henry that Tom and his wife, Lynn, visited

Medway for the first of many times. Tom's magnificent color photographs are combined with black and white photographs by such masters as Toni Frissell, as well as photographs from the Medway archives.

To reveal the essence of Medway, this book strives to present both its expansiveness and its exquisite detail. I also hope to present an "upstairs, downstairs" kind of perspective, having been privileged to sit at Gertrude's table for countless luncheons and dinner parties, while at the same time allowed to poke around the pantry and cellar with her gracious staff, or to accompany her manager on a controlled burn in the forest. Through photographs, interviews, letters, plantation records and diaries, the book offers a rare public viewing of three centuries of life on a private plantation–a life intimately intertwined with the landscape.

The main house is set among groves of tall, graceful live oaks (Quercus virginiana) whose limbs provide homes for epiphytes such as Spanish moss and resurrection fern.

Thus, the reader will find a melange of voices and images: a letter written by Elizabeth Hyrne painfully describing the fire that burned the first Medway house to the ground; slave descendant Willie Washington recalling his days as a woodcutter; Sidney Legendre's poignant diary of plantation life in the 30s and 40s; Bing Crosby's visit in 1965; hunt luncheons in the field; a dawn landing of thousands of ring-necked ducks on Crane Pond; and the Gourdine family returning to their ancestors' graves. The one voice that permeates Medway's story more than any other, however, is that of the individual who has lived there the longest–Gertrude Legendre. In spite of her insistence that this be a book about Medway and not herself, Gertrude's attachment to the land and animals and her passion for improving society have been the most powerful force behind Medway's preservation.

Today, you'll still find "Gertie" overseeing the plantation, engrossed in a book on the terrace, or down by the Home Reserve pond entertaining guests at the Log Cabin. Her petite frame belies her giant will. Having put away her shotgun in favor of a camera, she continues to compile scrapbooks and add to the record of the place that for 70 years she has called "home."

Whether you've known Medway all of your life or are a recent arrival, you sense immediately its power of place. Hervey Allen best described it in these lines from "Back River," a poem he wrote about Medway in 1922: "Something of its immortal live-oak sap suffuses Its sturdy men and houses…."

Opposite:
Gertrude Legendre, the mistress of Medway since 1929.

A BRAVE
PLANTATION

Fleeing his creditors in England, Edward Hyrne, a Norfolk merchant in his 40s, arrived in the Carolinas in 1700. His second wife, Elizabeth Massingbred, about 20 years old and daughter of a baronet, followed him to the New World against her family's wishes. The next year, Edward purchased Medway Plantation entirely on credit, counting on Elizabeth's share of her deceased father's estate to enable them to eventually pay off the debt. (Schmidt, 1961 & 1962)

Anxious, yet hopeful, Elizabeth wrote her brother in England:

...if you can git any of our friends to lend us one hundred pounds it would doe us a great kindness for we very much want slaves & we would pay them it with intrest in a very short time for had we a good stock of slaves we might in a littell time git a very good estate of our plantation having severall wayes to rais monys of it as rice & other provisions picth tar sedar syprus oake & other timber where of might be great sumes of mony raised....

Opportunities seemed limitless in Carolina, but the challenges were formidable to colonists like the Hyrnes. Charles Town was only 30 years old at the time and the colony was far from secure. The French and Spanish threatened its borders, and pirates plied its waterways. English enslavement of Indians, occupation of Indian lands and ill-regulated trade practices with the Native Americans created yet another adversary. The climate of uncertainty was exacerbated by the growth of the African slave trade. According to archaeologist Carl Steen, "By

I have likewise found credit for a brave plantation, wch I had bought...for £1,000 Carolina-Money: it consists of 2,550 Acres of land, whereof, 200 clear'd, & most fenc'd in, tho wants repairing; 150 Head of Cattle, 4 Horses, an Indian Slave almost a Man, a few Hogs, some Householdstuff, & the best Brick-House in all the Country; built about 9 years ago, & cost £700, 80 Foot long, 26 broad, cellar'd throughout.

Edward Hyrne,
Charles-Town
Jan. 19th, 1701

1708, planters had imported so many Africans that they constituted a majority of the population." Historians estimate that more than a third of all African-Americans are descended from African slaves who arrived in Charleston.

The physical environment was hostile as well. The average life span of a South Carolinian in 1750 was 45 years–about the age at which Medway's first owner succumbed. Dysentery, malaria and yellow fever plagued the colonists. Of the Anglican missionaries who came to South Carolina in the 18th century, over half either died or fell seriously ill within ten years. (Weir, 1983)

Yet the lure of owning land kept settlers like the Hyrnes coming. Edward Hyrne bought Medway from Thomas Smith II, who had inherited the plantation from his father, Thomas Smith of Exeter, England. The elder Smith belonged to a group of well-educated Baptists and Presbyterians who dissented from the Church of England. At the time, several publications promoted Carolina as a haven for "Dissenters" like Smith. Despite his affiliations, Smith eventually became a landgrave and governor of the province.

Son Thomas wrote about his family's emigration to America: "In the year 1683 my father freighted a ship from Dartmouth bound for Carolina where we arrived in 4 or 5 months time." The following year, his father purchased from the Lords Proprietors 400 acres of land fronting on the Back River. This parcel would become the core parcel of Medway Plantation and the site of its present house. (Côté, 1993)

The Medway name originated from Back River's former name of "Meadway River," which was identified in Smith's 1693 certificate of survey and appears on several early plats. "Mead" and "medwa" were Old English words for meadow; and in southeast England a Medway River flows through Kent into the Thames at Sheerness.

At the time of Landgrave Smith's arrival, settlers in Carolina were entitled to receive warrants for land based on the number of persons immigrating. The head of household was entitled to a grant of 150 acres, plus an additional 50 acres for each family member, servant or slave. In the language of the time, the term "grant" designated the legal instrument by which ownership of land was conferred by the sovereign. (Côté, 1993)

In 1663, King Charles II of England granted the land known as Carolina to eight Lords Proprietors. The Lords Proprietors offered incentives of land ownership to prospective Carolina immigrants in order to establish a North American colony that would provide valuable raw materials directly to the mother country. These raw materials would be exchanged for English manufactured goods, desper-

Landgrave Thomas Smith II, a governor of the Carolina colony and early owner of Medway. His father's gravesite, as seen in an 1875 view from Harper's New Monthly Magazine, *has been restored by the Legendres.*

ately needed by a fledgling colony such as Carolina and useful in trading with the Indians.

This arrangement was similar to that between England and the Caribbean island of Barbados. In reality, Charleston and South Carolina's tidewater plantations were more closely tied to Europe and the Caribbean than to their surrounding region. The "plantation" and its slave economy, though akin to Europe's feudal order, really grew out of the Caribbean colonial scene. Some of the Lowcountry's first settlers came from Barbados with their slaves and helped establish the plantation system in South Carolina.

Smith obtained a warrant for a grant of 650 acres as his arrival right in 1684 but quickly divested himself of it. The land was located on the Wadmalaw River, south of Charleston. Its proximity to the ocean, with all the uncertainties of a maritime environment, may have persuaded Smith to sell the land and instead purchase 400 acres at Medway, along the fresher, safer reaches of the Cooper River.

Not long after Smith's purchase of Medway, his

The river facade of the main house as illustrated in Harper's New Monthly Magazine *(1875).*

first wife died. In 1688, he married Sabina de Vignon van Aerssen, the childless, 46-year-old widow of Johan van Aerssen, South Carolina's first Dutch immigrant. Smith's marriage to van Aerrsen's widow enabled him to increase his landholdings considerably. Van Aerrsen's Dutch nobility had allowed him to petition the Lords Proprietors for the right to claim 12,000 acres of land over and above his basic arrival rights. The Proprietors awarded the claim to van Aerrsen in 1686 along with "all the Privileges of a Barony."

After the nobleman's death and Smith's marriage to his widow, not only did Smith successfully acquire van Aerssen's arrival rights through his wife's inheritance, but he also won the right to van Aerssen's barony. One of Smith's first claims to a portion of the Dutchman's grant was a request for 2,100 acres adjoining his 400 acres at Medway. These two parcels formed the bulk of the plantation's acreage when it was sold by Smith's son to Edward Hyrne in 1701. (Côté, 1993)

By 1703, the Hyrnes were still waiting on wife Elizabeth's inheritance. Then a series of tragedies struck the family. Elizabeth wrote home early in 1704:

On the 20 of the same instant [June] we lost a Negro Man by the bite of a rattlesnake which was a very great lose to us being just in the height of weeding…[torn] rice. On the 25 of August I lost my Dear little son which went very near to me. In September we lost our Cattle hunter. But the greatest of all our losses (except my dear Harry) was on the 12 day on Janwery last on which we was burn…[torn] out of all our house taking fire I know not how in the night and burned so fircely that we had much to do to save the life of poor burry [Burrell, their son] and two beds just to lye on which was the cheif of what we saved we also had all our rice and corn and all sorts of our provehons burnt. Cloes and every thing nothing escapted the fire so that if it had not bin for some good peaple we must have perished. My dear child was forced to be taken naked out of bed being left without close enough to keep him from the cold. And now I am big with Child expecting to lye inn the beginning of next June so that you may easely imaging our messarable condission. But blessed be God we have mett with some kind friends in this place or elce we had not bin for you ever to have heard more of us. For it is impossible for you to think how sad a thing it is to be burnt out of all in a nights time.

Undaunted, the Hyrnes had built a smaller version of the original brick house by the following year, but when Edward returned to England to claim his wife's inheritance, his creditors threw him in

The main house is flanked by smaller dependencies which were added to the complex over a 200-year period.

Built in the first decade of the 1700s, Medway is the oldest extant masonry structure in the Carolinas.

prison. Shipwrecked and rescued en route, Elizabeth followed her husband to England. Tragically, the family failed to make a single payment on Medway and, in 1711, it reverted to Thomas Smith II, ending the Hyrne family's aspirations for their "brave plantation."

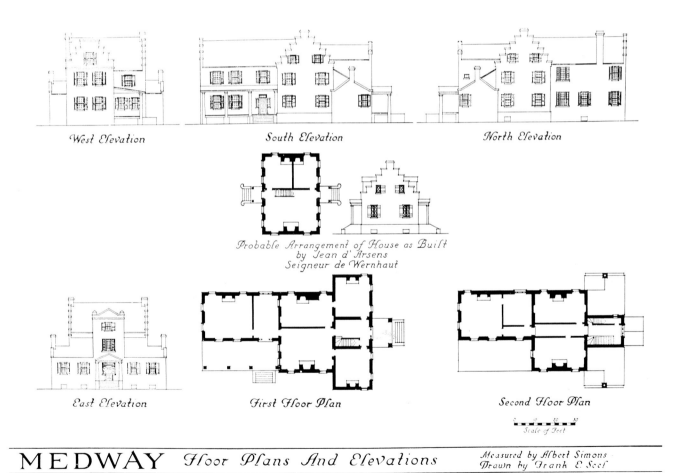

West Elevation

South Elevation

North Elevation

Probable Arrangement of House as Built
by Jean d' Arsens
Seigneur de Wernhaut

East Elevation

First Floor Plan

Second Floor Plan

Scale of Feet

MEDWAY *Floor Plans And Elevations*

Measured by Albert Simons
Drawn by Frank E. Seel

A QUAINT AND ANCIENT MANSION

The Hyrnes would quite literally leave an indelible mark on Medway. Their letters, discovered around 1960 in Elizabeth's birthplace of Lincolnshire, England, established crucial events and dates in Medway's early history, especially pertaining to the house. In the summer of 1984, a main support wall in the center of the present house collapsed, confirming at last the identity of its builder.

It all began with a sticking door between the hall and the pantry. When plantation manager Bob Hortman investigated, he discovered that the wall around the doorway was collapsing. He decided to further expose the wall to get a better look. On the appointed day, historian Agnes Baldwin observed as Bob and his crew began ripping out plaster. "It was the hottest day in the world," Agnes remembered, "and we didn't know what to expect." Beneath all the plaster and wires, they began to find evidence of an exterior wall–stucco, pointed bricks, windows and doors. The footings and mortar were gone, but the wooden sills and frame, rotten with age, remained around the bricked-in openings.

Then Bob and the workmen noticed something peculiar about several bricks around the doorway. Each one had been stamped with what looked like a stationery seal, about the size of a nickel. Someone brought out a magnifying glass. The stamp was a coat of arms.

They cleaned and photographed the impression and Agnes researched the identity of the family. After poring through registries of armorial bearings at the Charleston Library Society, she discovered that the coat of arms belonged to the Hyrnes. "When it matched, it was really amazing," she recalled. "I had suspected that this was the original Hyrne house, but I never dreamed of such a confirmation."

"I couldn't help but remember Elizabeth Hyrne's letter," Agnes said, "asking her brother in England to send them their cup, ring and spoons, and one 'cote of arms.'" Perhaps in response to having lost everything in the fire, the Hyrnes were determined to impress their family name, literally and indelibly, upon the walls of the second Medway. In addition to the seals, charred remains of hand-hewn floor joists were found embedded in the second-story bricks, lending evidence to the theory that the Hyrnes rebuilt Medway using the original walls and foundation of the 1692 house that burned.

The Hyrne family coat of arms found stamped on bricks in the main house.

Furthermore, a 1792 plat shows that there were once two flanking structures on each side of the river entrance to the house. In 1993 and 1994, archaeologist Carl Steen discovered a brick foundation of one of these structures as well as shards of 18th century Delftware, creamware and lead-glazed slipware on the site. The artifacts indicate a domestic use for the flanker, but more excavation will be needed to fully explore its function and construction. (Steen, 1996)

Historians are not completely sure how Medway evolved from a small, one-and-a-half story, home-made brick house to the "quaint and ancient mansion" author John Bennett described 200 years later. The off-center west wing is known to have been added in 1855 by Peter Gaillard Stoney. But the date and builder of the east wing and its stair tower, the second full story and the famed stepped gables are unknown. Historians do know that the house had assumed its present arrangement by 1875, confirmed by a drawing of Medway that appeared that year in *Harper's New Monthly Magazine.*

As a result, it is impossible to "size Medway up" at a glance. From every angle, a different configuration emerges. For many, the gabled roof recalls Medway's Dutch beginnings, while its stair tower and wings appear reminiscent of an English manor house. (Stockton, 1981) Architectural historian Gene Waddell wrote in 1979 that the central hall and piazza-like side terrace seemed "strikingly Charlestonian." And from dawn to dusk, light and shadow filtered by the live oaks play upon Medway's old pink walls, adding yet another degree of complexity to what Robert Stockton describes as an "architectural puzzle."

As historian Sam Stoney wrote, the harmonious whole that is Medway is indeed "a triumph of style over circumstance."

CHANGING
FORTUNES

After the Hyrnes lost Medway in 1711, Thomas Smith offered it for sale to Abraham Satur, the first of a long succession of owners which included James Hasell, James Wathen, Thomas Wright, Aaron Loocock, Thomas Drayton and John Bee Holmes. Holmes failed to pay the taxes on the property, and in 1827, Medway was sold at a sheriff's sale to Theodore Samuel Marion, nephew of Revolutionary War General Francis Marion. Marion died that same year and left the property to his grandson, Theodore Samuel DuBose. DuBose then sold Medway to his brother-in-law, Peter Gaillard Stoney, between 1833 and 1835. The Stoneys remained at Medway for the next 100 years. (Côté, 1993)

DuBose and Stoney were married to the Porcher sisters, Jane and Anna. To these two sisters, "Medway owes its planting of trees," Medway descendant Sam Stoney, Jr. wrote. "The larger oaks about the house were set out by Mrs. Theodore Marion DuBose, mistress of the plantation from 1825 to 1835. Mrs. Peter Gaillard Stoney set out the double avenue in 1855."

While drawing on English traditions of symmetry and order, the sisters' choice of plantings and design bore a distinctively Lowcountry flavor. The live oak, in particular, with its "gnarled and ponderous branches, the squat, thick, deeply lined trunk, the rank growth of moss and tree ferns"–as described by Edward Shaffer in his book *Carolina Gardens*–symbolized both the wildness and endurance of the New World.

DuBose Heyward, author of *Porgy* and a friend of the later generation of Stoneys, expounded on the New World gardens of early Carolina in his foreword to Shaffer's book: "...far from Europe with its ingrained traditions, its pride of caste and place, surrounded by many freedoms, by vast spaces, by new majestic trees and luxuriant flowers...no more would gardens in such an atmosphere obey meticulous laws....The ordered terrace, the mount, the statues were soon subordinated to a more gracious exposition of the landscape, a glorification of trees, an acceptance of the flowers."

Bricks from the abandoned rice mill were reused in the restoration of the Medway gardens.

Meanwhile, Peter Stoney continued the conversion of Medway's natural resources into large-scale agricultural and industrial enterprises. He was a rice planter and by 1860 had 120 slaves working at Medway and other landholdings in the parish of St. James, Goose Creek. (Côté, 1993)

From March through September, the slaves cultivated rice, which had become the major crop in the area and its greatest source of wealth. The slaves also raised corn, potatoes, peas, groundnuts and oats, as well as livestock. In the fall and winter, they made bricks.

Historians believe that Medway prospered largely because of its river frontage and its good clay for brickmaking. Slaves mined Medway's generous clay reserves to produce fireproof building materials for construction in Charleston. The city had suffered from a series of major fires, prompting the General Assembly to require the outside of all buildings in Charleston to be built of brick or stone. (Wayne, 1992)

In one day–October 9, 1852–an overseer's daybook for Medway reports that 12 slaves produced 6,000 bricks: "2 hands digging clay"; "1 hand carting clay to pit"; "1 hand filling pit"; "6 hands cutting wood, hauling wood, moulding bricks"; "1 hand putting out fire"; "1 hand loading bricks under shed." Peter set up the brickmaking operation adjacent to his landing on the Back River, just south of Medway house. He owned a sloop on which he transported his bricks to Charleston via Back River and the Cooper River into Charleston Harbor. In a ten-month period from 1852 to 1853, Peter shipped 594,000 bricks, and according to Sam Stoney, "sent thousands down to the building of famous Fort Sumter." Sam also wrote that Medway brick was used to build nearby Dean Hall as well as several houses in downtown Charleston.

Today, the old burrow pits, kilns and wells are covered by forest. Also hidden in the trees some 75 yards from the Back River landing lies a tremendous steam boiler. Approximately 30 feet long, made of solid steel and weighing probably 15 tons, it looks like a submarine beached in the woods. Similar in size to a boiler for rice pounding, Medway's boiler may have powered a brickmaking machine like the one believed to have been used at Boone Hall Plantation by the Horlbeck family. In Medway's brickmaking area, one finds both handmade bricks—typically larger, softer and more irregular—and machine-made bricks, which are smaller and more compressed. (Wayne, 1992)

Timber cutting was also a lucrative trade and no doubt much of the virgin pine and cypress at Medway was sawn and sold for lumber. Longleaf

A rare view of the main house (right) drawn by author John Bennett in 1900 and the plantation school house as seen in Harper's New Monthly Magazine, *1875.*

pines, such as those at Medway, framed and floored most of the early houses in Carolina while cypress panelled the walls. At various times, Medway engaged in the production of "naval stores" as well. Throughout the woods one finds circular, doughnut-shaped mounds, or "tar pits," where longleaf pine was burned in order to collect the resin found in the inner bark. The gummy residue was sold to shipbuilders to seal hulls and caulk decks; it was also used for thinning paints and even for making soap.

In the last half of the 19th century, however, a civil war, an earthquake and a series of hurricanes brought Medway to its knees. Peter Stoney and six of his sons, like so many southern families, fought for the Confederacy. Its defeat in 1865 marked the end of the prosperous South Carolina rice culture and the onset of an economic collapse that would afflict the region for decades.

The 1886 earthquake that shook Charleston and the surrounding area caused substantial damage to Medway's house. By 1900, the house had been repaired and outfitted with "earthquake bolts," which are still visible today. The iron rods, each one culminating in a large washer and nut, ran the length of the house and were actually rotated to resquare the structure and pull it back into shape. (Côté, 1993)

The roof gables, which had been "thrown down in the earthquake," were later put back by Captain Samuel Gaillard Stoney, who bought Medway from his Uncle Peter's family in 1906. Captain Stoney was a rice planter and president of the West Point Mill in Charleston that eventually closed because of the decline of the rice industry. For 15 years, he served as president of the Agricultural Society of South Carolina and worked, in particular, on converting abandoned ricefields to new crops. The title by which he was familiarly known was the result of sev-

eral years of service as a captain of the Charleston
Light Dragoons, a local militia company dating back
to colonial times.

Captain Stoney described moving to Medway on
Thanksgiving Day in 1906: "Moved over from
'Cottage' [at neighboring Parnassus Plantation] to
'Medway' this day. The ladies Mrs. David G. Stoney,
Miss Frances G. Harrison, the two Miss Cheves',
Harriet and Louisa Stoney assisted by Mrs. Cheves
Smythe, Charley Cheves, Sam Stoney Jr. and
Augustine Stoney arranged the moving, putting
'Medway' house in order, hung pictures etc. On
Monday after Thanksgiving Mr. John Bennett, Miss
S. H. Smythe and Mrs. Sam G. Stoney spent two
days laying out and planting the flower garden on
the site formerly occupied by the flower garden of
Mrs. P. Gaillard Stoney. Mr. S. Dwight Stoney had
planted a small flower garden on the west of the
dwelling about 1895: a few Azaleas (Roses) and a
variety of bulbs were flourishing when we moved
into 'Medway.' Work on cleaning up Avenues etc.
was commenced at once."

Despite having fallen on hard times after the
Civil War, Medway became well known as a hunting
retreat. "The living, or hunters' room is a marvel in
its display of deer horns," wrote a hunting guest in
1912, "the walls being encircled by row upon row of
them, possibly 300. These were all taken in the
manly sport each season indulged in at Medway by
Captain Stoney and his friends. The covering of the
floor is deer robes or skins."

On entering an adjoining room, this same guest
encountered "Confederate souvenirs, muskets, can-
teens, knapsacks, portraits, etc." They dined on
"…delicious cooter soup, roasted duck, juicy venison
haunch, roasted oysters, sherry, wine, etc. etc."
Outside, by the river entrance, was a wood pile
stacked ten to twelve feet high for stoking several

fireplaces within.

Captain Stoney's wife, Louisa Smythe, grand-daughter of conservative intellectual Louisa McCord and affectionately known as "Miss Lou," carried out the restoration of Medway's gardens and grounds and laid out the terraces and flowering shrubs between the avenues of oaks. She found fewer than a dozen azalea plants when she arrived at Medway in 1906, and by 1930 she had left 700. Miss Lou wrote in 1935, "For fully twenty years I worked...under the

Captain Samuel Gaillard Stoney and his wife, Louisa, spent 20 years reclaiming the ancient gardens and planting new gardens.

Lowcountry authors DuBose Heyward and Hervey Allen with "Miss Lou" digging up a Medway tree to send to poet Amy Lowell, ca. 1920s.

oak trees of the plantation of Medway, then the property of my husband, Samuel Gaillard Stoney. My especial interest was in the reclaiming of old and planting new gardens, as well as landscaping the avenue leading to the house."

Miss Lou's grandson Stoney Simons, born in 1920, remembers the "clean-swept" sand paths of his grandmother's garden. He also remembers many evenings spent by the fire at Medway, there being no central heat or electricity. They drew water from a deep well next to the house and used two brick privies outside by the kitchen garden, one for the ladies and one for the gentlemen. Special guests were provided with a chamber pot.

"I remember there always being a house full of people. The children would be sent to sleep on the third floor, which we were convinced was haunted," Stoney recalls. Over in the garage, he and his young cousins would marvel at two rattlesnake skins that hung from the rafters, sewn up and stuffed with sand, stretching some nine feet to the ground.

"Most of my memories of Medway are outside," Stoney says. "My grandfather would take me on long horseback rides, sitting me in front of him on the saddle from which a Winchester rifle usually hung. He wore a jacket, corduroy trousers and boots, and often carried along his box camera.

"The roads could be very bad. I remember ten cars stuck in the mud at once. There were long stretches of what we called 'corduroy road,' where saplings were cut and laid side-by-side across low spots, creating a kind of corduroy effect.

"My mother used to tell me that more than once after a dance in Charleston, when she and her brothers were young, they would leave the city on horseback and ride the 25 miles to Medway in the dark of night. They all had good voices and in later years, I can remember them singing spirituals under Medway's live oaks in the moonlight.

"One of my most terrifying memories was being hauled out of the house in the middle of the night to help fight a wild fire in the forest. We children were given the job of sweeping pine needles and other debris off the road to prevent the fire from spreading across it. The sound of the roaring blaze was deafening."

Indeed, Medway's house, its people and its landscape touched the lives of the Stoney family in profound ways. Miss Lou's paintings and prize-winning poetry often centered on plantation life–the black families, the live oaks, the forest, the swamp. Her obituary in 1939 identified her as a "Friend of the Negro," because of her many civic activities on behalf of Charleston's African Americans. In 1932, she edited and expanded John Irving's *A Day on Cooper River*, the much quoted 19th century chronicle of some 70 plantations, including Medway, along the historic Cooper River.

Miss Lou's son Augustine, a land surveyor, also wrote poetry and was well known for his sketches and illustrated maps of the Lowcountry. Her sister Susan married writer John Bennett, whose book *The Treasure of Peyre Gaillard*, published in 1906, was set at Medway. Written on a dare from Miss Lou and dedicated to the Stoneys, the book was "an account of the recovery on a South Carolina Plantation, of a Treasure, which had Remained Buried and Lost in a Vast Swamp for over a Hundred Years."

Like her mother, Miss Lou's daughter Harriet was active in civic affairs. She married local architect Albert Simons, who together with her brother, Sam Stoney, Jr., wrote *Plantations of the Carolina Low Country*, a book that did much to inspire the preservation of places like Medway. In fact, Simons oversaw renovations to the house both in 1912 and in 1930.

Sam Jr., also an architect, became a renowned preservationist, author and storyteller. His novels *Black Genesis* and *Po' Buckra* drew from the Gullah traditions passed down by Medway's slave descendants. In a letter to his uncle, John Bennett, Sam described the writing of *Black Genesis*: "We [he and Gertrude Shelby] have taken liberties with the stories and we have modified the dialect, but I have been doing my darnedest to give it the swing of the narrative and the construction and action that Davy [David Gourdine of Medway], for instance, put into his stuff."

Henry Lowndes, whose parents were friends with the Stoneys, recalls visiting Medway around 1920 with his father:

We traveled on a winding country road through the

Author John Bennett and wife Susan Smythe Bennett (foreground) with friends at Medway in the spring of 1927. Bennett's popular novel The Treasure of Peyre Gaillard, *published in 1906, was set at Medway.*

pine land. The avenue was grown up with bushes and the house was badly in need of repairs.

When we got to the house, we were greeted by David Gourdine, who knew my Father and worked for Captain Stoney. We entered the house by the rear or the river side and went through a hall into a small room that smelled of stale ashes; for many a fire had been made there over the years. There was no furniture except for a few tables and broken chairs.

We stood by the fire and chatted for some time; my Father picking up stories he would dress up and retell. Before we left, we went to see the grave of Landgrave Smith. There was a brick enclosure with a gravestone which was broken almost in half. David explained to us that this was done by a runaway mule and wagon.

Several years later, I returned on horseback and as I approached the house, I found it and the grounds in the same condition as on my previous visit. As I was riding away, I glanced back at the old house and thought how majestic it looked and what a shame it was that it was left to go to ruin. Never did I believe that I would live to see it restored to its original splendor.

After Captain Stoney died in 1926, the family struggled to maintain their beloved hunting grounds. They tried leasing the property, as well as timbering and raising cattle. Sam Jr. was heard more than once to say "Lord, please send us a rich Yankee," and in 1929 his prayer was answered. That year, Miss Lou and her children—Sam, Augustine, Harriet and Louisa—sold their "Back River" Plantation to Gertrude and Sidney Legendre for $100,000. At the time, Medway consisted of 2,530 acres, just 20 acres shy of the total acreage the Hyrnes purchased in 1701.

The loss for the family was great, as evidenced by a letter written by daughter Louisa Popham to her mother a month before the sale: "I won't even mention Back River because we all know how we all feel." Sam wrote three weeks later about the celebrated deer horns on Medway's living room walls: "…I think it would be a safe rule to make to let anybody named Stoney take their horns away."

"Even as a child, I sensed the tremendous loss to my family when Medway was sold," Stoney Simons recalls. "It was an intense and deep affiliation. Medway had been such a unifying and rallying place for all of us."

Today, near the mouth of the Cooper River in Charleston, one can visit the graves of Miss Lou and Captain Stoney at Magnolia Cemetery. Though a good distance downriver from Medway, the epitaph on Captain Stoney's gravestone recalls the legacy of their beloved plantation: "…let his dear land keep fresh the impulse of the love he gave."

The idyllic garden, also known as "Grandmother's Garden."

A NEW LANDED SOCIETY

In October of 1929, Ben Kittredge invited newly-weds Gertrude and Sidney Legendre to visit Dean Hall Plantation on the Cooper River, 25 miles northeast of Charleston. The Kittredges were old family friends from Aiken and New York. Ben Kittredge, Sr., a noted preservationist and creator of Cypress Gardens, had purchased and restored Dean Hall in the early 1900s. Mrs. Kittredge had been born and raised in Charleston.

Gertrude and Sidney were motoring down the southeast coast looking for a place to settle. Gertrude was born on March 29, 1902, in Aiken, South Carolina, where her parents migrated each winter from their home at Amsterdam, New York. She recalls her impressions on returning to South Carolina to visit the Kittredges: "I was back in the state where I was born, and I was falling in love all over again with its warmth and charm.

"One morning during our visit, our hosts suggested we ride horses over to neighboring Medway Plantation (which was for sale at the time) and have a picnic. We started down the old Cypress Garden Road, which was dirt, then turned into Spring Grove Plantation, crossed the Back River, and followed the dirt trails across Pine Grove Plantation.

"As we neared Medway, I remember peering under a festoon of gray moss dripping from huge oak trees and catching sight of an old, eerie pink structure. The setting was weird and mysterious. It reminded me of one of Arthur Rackham's drawings.

I known Medway since the Stoney time. I was just a boy and I visit my great-grandmother Pearson Green there. She live in the kitchen house by the big oak tree. I live on Cypress Garden Road, in a board house with a brick chimney. I walk across Black River, then walk the railroad tracks to visit. [Some African Americans use the name "Black" River instead of Back River.]

We pick up pecans, hickory nuts, and walnuts from right in the yard and we drink buttermilk from the cow. We cook in a iron frying pan and a iron pot over the fire—corn bread, cow peas, black molasses.

When I start courtin' Miss Maggie Gourdine, her father David and her mother Candace live in the house near where Mr. Legendre is buried now, where the cedar tree was. We was married there around 1920. It cost $1.50 for the preacher and $1.75 for the license.

"We circled the building on our horses. Brick steps led to the east door of the Back River entrance. I could see remains of a derelict avenue of oaks leading to the river. Inside, mattresses covered the floor, and deer horns adorned the walls. There was no water, no light, no heat.

"In the yard was an outhouse and a pile of pine logs for the open fireplaces. That was all. I remember seeing two black women, one of whom was Candace Gourdine, widow of David, who lived with her children in a frame cabin not far from the main house.

"Below the house, the lake was invisible, hidden by a mass of pine and myrtle. We ate our sandwiches on the causeway by the old rice trunk and rode on to

Gertrude and Sidney Legendre with "Clippy" in 1929.

36

the next door plantation, known as Parnassus. We saw evidence of an old house site by the river and a magnificent avenue of oaks. On our way home, we returned for another glimpse of Medway; the old pink house was pulling Sidney and me under its spell.

"Back at Dean Hall that evening, we talked over our day's expedition. 'What fun it would be,' said Ben, Jr., 'if you bought Medway and we all lived like neighbors here, shooting and fishing and enjoying life in the Lowcountry.' Sidney and I agreed."

The young couple left Dean Hall and completed their tour through South Carolina and Georgia before heading to Palm Beach to visit Gertrude's father, John Sanford. Mr. Sanford directed the family's carpet business in Amsterdam, New York, that his grandfather founded in 1842. He also owned Hurricana, the celebrated horse-breeding farm in Amsterdam begun by his father. Gertrude's mother, Ethel Sanford, a second cousin of Gertrude's father, had died in 1924. When the market crashed in 1929, the Sanfords had very little of their money in stocks and according to Gertrude, "the misery of much of the world was unknown to us."

Mr. Sanford considered the Lowcountry unhealthy for a permanent home and believed his daughter and son-in-law were crazy not to want to settle near him in either New York or Palm Beach. Gertrude says emphatically, "Sidney and I both loved the out-of-doors and neither of us had any desire for city life. We desperately wanted to live in the country, where one is close to nature and far from the surge of traffic and people."

"I guess we were rash and romantic enough to think we could tackle Medway," reflects Gertrude. "In the end, my father agreed to help us purchase the house and some 2500 acres from the Stoney family for $100,000. From then on, there was plenty to do

I farm with mules and a plow—corn, lespedeza, and millet. I drive the mule to the corn mill and the rice mill. I build barbed wire fence and I cut wood. I been 60 years at Medway. I been to every corner, been to all the corner posts, all up and down the road.

When Mrs. Legendre and Mr. Legendre come to see the place, come shopping to see the house, he and Madam hold hands, and walk, and walk, and walk. They say, "Good mornin'." We say, "Good mornin' Boss. Good mornin' Madam." Then Mr. Legendre say, "Look here boys, I want but two or three of your good men, but I ain't want no men from Charleston, no men from Charleston…I want that man, and I want him, and I want him."

They say Mr. Stoney say later, "Take care of the Gourdines. Take the best care you can of 'em."
Willie Washington, Medway
September 16, 1996

The Legendres in the Medway rice fields. They took courses at Cornell to prepare for the rigors of restoring the plantation.

and plenty to think about."

The Legendres and the Kittredges were not alone in their appreciation of the Lowcountry. They were part of a large migration of wealthy northerners to South Carolina that began as early as the 1880s and continued into the 1940s. According to geographer Charles Kovacik, many factors came together at the turn of the century to propel this "second northern invasion": the accumulation of great sums of wealth in the North, the availability of large tracts of land in the South, the growth of the railroad and the development of the modern shotgun, which led to greater popularity of "wing shooting."

"During this period, well over 100 South Carolina plantations were bought by wealthy northerners and managed as shooting preserves," says Kovacik. "Originally, they leased the land for very little and secured shooting rights in perpetuity, traveling by train to visit. Then they began purchasing the plantations outright."

The new plantation owners persuaded other influential industrialists and financiers from the North and Midwest to join them. Names such as Vanderbilt, Pulitzer, Guggenheim, Field, Whitney, duPont, Dodge, Roosevelt, Hutton, Pratt, Baruch, Yawkey, Knoth, Huntington, Winthrop, Luce and Milbank began to appear on deeds of sale up and down the South Carolina coast. By virtue of their large landholdings, commitment to conservation and good timber and game management, they preserved vast tracts of healthy forest, swamp and gamelands that today distinguish South Carolina.

Writing for *Country Life* in January 1932, James Derieux described the lure of the Lowcountry in an article entitled "The Renaissance of the Plantation":

When the Legendres moved to Medway in 1930, they found plantation life both exhilarating and challenging. Dirt roads, few phones and even fewer cars underscored a feeling of being on a frontier.

40

"There is no part of America more remote from pressure salesmanship and its philosophy of hurry and shove; there is no place where the sound of a stock ticker would seem so ill-suited to the surroundings. Any one stopping for a few minutes beside a silent coastal stream, or gazing at a majestic oak, can understand the love of the Northerner for the balmy silence of the old rice scenes."

Derieux told his readers that "It was the hunter who really first 'discovered' the charm of the Carolina coast. He found there plenty of deer, turkeys, ducks, and quail. He invited his friends, and they in turn bought places for themselves. They invited their friends, and thus the redemption of the Lowcountry got under way."

The quail hunters, in particular, generated new jobs associated with their extensive kennels and stables, and the maintenance of their houses, plantation lands and rather refined lifestyle. This influx of wealth contrasted sharply with South Carolina's paralyzed rural economy. In 1929, the median per capita income in South Carolina was $269, and the state's illiteracy rate of nearly 15 percent was the highest in the nation. Berkeley County, where Medway is situated, suffered terribly during the Depression, with only about one third of its population gainfully employed.

Thus, when the Legendres moved to Medway in 1930, they found plantation life both exhilarating and challenging. Dirt roads, few phones and even fewer cars underscored a feeling of being on a frontier of sorts. Sidney, a native of New Orleans and a descendant of rice planters, was unquestionably a southerner. Nevertheless, his Princeton education, coupled with his mother's Philadelphia roots and Gertrude's New York ancestry, gave him compelling insights into the worlds of both North and South. He wrote the following observation in his diary:

Opposite:
"As we neared Medway, I remember peering under a festoon of gray moss dripping from huge oak trees and catching sight of an old, eerie pink structure....the old pink house was pulling Sidney and me under its spell."

One cannot understand at first the curious air of dilapidation that always lies over the south. At first the northerner's impulse is to start cleaning and tidying things up. He works until his very soul cries out and then straightening his back he looks around with an expression of delight in his eyes to think he has conquered the country. How quickly that expression changes to one of bewilderment. How suddenly the happiness flies his face leaving an expression of unalterable gloom. True he had been told that the moment he had finished one thing and turned his back on it, it would return to disorder and decay. But he had thought that was only southern talk and southern laziness. It is not. Born in the body, bred in the bone of the south is the spirit of decay. Books mildew, dogs and horses are infected with worms. Walls run water with moisture, machinery rots in spite of care.

The Legendres began their first task—refurbishing the old house—with the help of Charleston architect Albert Simons, son-in-law of Captain Stoney. Gertrude recalls those days vividly: "We rented a house on Church Street in downtown Charleston and spent the winter with lawyers, contractors and architects while we made daily visits to Medway to oversee its renovation. When we finally moved in, workmen were everywhere. Everything seemed delayed. Tomorrow cement would come to lay the bricks for the walks, tomorrow this, tomorrow that; I thought it would never end.

"We were busy every minute, planning, putting furniture in place, and unpacking boxes of wedding presents—wonderful wedding presents, because we were married before the Crash of '29 and Mother's friends had given us beautiful things. Sidney's brother Morris gave us our Tiffany flat silver, and other friends gave us glass and linen; now we were ready to put it all to use. How lucky we were."

Meanwhile, the Legendres were expanding Medway's acreage. To the original 2,530 acres pur-

Opposite:
Interior woodwork includes antique cypress panels used as decorative wall finish.

chased from the Stoney family, they added Pine Grove and Spring Grove Plantations. By 1934, the "new" Medway totaled 7,110 acres.

"From the house at Pine Grove, we removed cypress paneling to install in the living room at Medway," Gertrude remembers. "We left Medway's rooms exactly where they were and concentrated on

making the house more livable while preserving the exterior as it was." Sidney commented in his diary on the process of "recycling" old structures:

The negroes live on in their tiny cabins around what was once their master's old home stealing tidbits of wood and brick so that they hasten the end that they already deplore. Gradually the house crumbles and falls to the ground and the vine that had caused its downfall creeps over it, and dust is blown in it so that in the end there is only a mound where once there has been a home.

How well I know these deaths. I had just finished causing one myself. The old rice mill that had stood on the banks of the Medway River for the past two hundred years had been pulled down under my orders. Its bricks had been carried to Medway and were now in the process of arising anew in the form of a wall around our vegetable garden. The old ragged edge slate from its roof was already on our stable and the time darkened beams and boards of its floors supported the roof and supplied the floors for the main arch and its room in the garden wall.

Dutch architect Ides Van Der Gracht designed the garden restoration using the bricks from the rice mill to which Sidney referred in his diary. Van Der Gracht set a greenhouse at the north end with a gabled roof resembling the one on the house; a serpentine wall along the west side (copied from Thomas Jefferson's garden walls at the University of Virginia); a Charleston wall on the east side; and a flanker at the southwest corner, which Gertrude used as a darkroom. Called a "kitchen garden" by the Stoneys, it was first planted in vegetables, then flowers, and finally returned to vegetables, which Gertrude found "far more practical and rewarding."

"Grandmother's Garden," also known as "Miss Lou's Garden," remained a showcase for flowers. "When we first came, its winding paths were overgrown and couldn't be seen," remembered Gertrude. "Mrs. Shipman [Ellen Biddle Shipman], a landscape

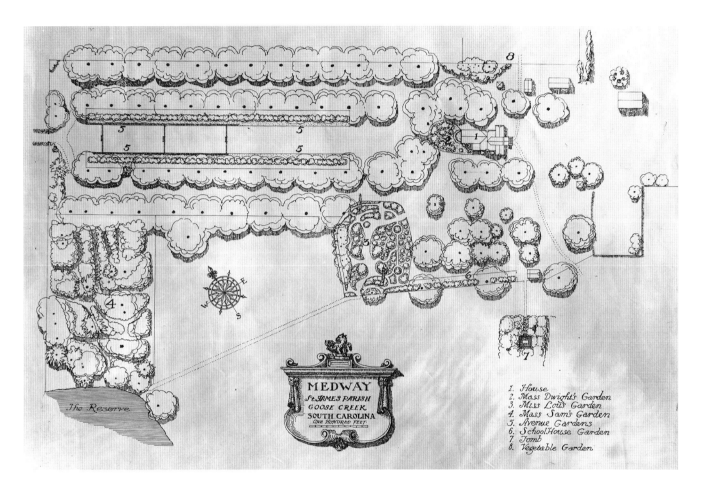

1. House
2. Mass Dwight's Garden
3. Miss Lou's Garden
4. Mass Sam's Garden
5. Avenue Gardens
6. School House Garden
7. Tomb
8. Vegetable Garden.

Dutch architect Ides Van Der Gracht was commissioned by the Legendres to plan the garden restoration.

gardener and friend of my mother's in New York, came down to Medway and on her hands and knees redefined the walks where they once were. We also added more trees and shrubs and bulbs, and later expanded the garden."

The agrarian ideal of the nobility of country life infused the refined, yet rustic lifestyle that Gertrude and Sidney cultivated at Medway. A working plantation was Sidney's dream. During the summer of 1941, they enrolled in agriculture school, a venture Sidney described in his diary:

July and half of August was spent at Cornell Agriculture School studying farm management, field machinery repair, and electricity....Gertrude studied nutrition and automobiles and their engines, and between the two of us we learned enough theoretical knowledge to run any farm successfully. Unfortunately farms are not run on theoretical knowledge but on experience and hard work. Neither of these two virtues are inherent in me, nor do either of us know them except by hearsay.

Nevertheless, they experimented with a myriad of crops and livestock on the plantation—rice, barley, wheat, corn, benne seed, rye, potatoes, poultry, hogs and cows—and eventually with the guidance of Bill Baldwin determined that Medway's clay soil was best suited for the production of timber. Sidney lamented that the work never seemed finished and likened his dread of returning to Medway after a summer away to the hopelessness and terror felt by the hapless victims of the 1889 flood in Johnstown, Pennsylvania. Another day, however, he wrote:

...I knew joys that I could not possibly have known elsewhere. I shall never be able to express clearly whence comes this pleasure derived from labor and worry, but I have seen men attach themselves more stubbornly to a difficult job than to any other.

The tremendous energy that the young couple poured into their plantation developed within them an almost inexplicable attachment to and passion for it. "We lived as if on an island," Gertrude remembers, "absorbed by daily events." Rather than becoming isolated, however, they were inspired to create a rich social life at Medway that was full of fun and purpose.

The enclosed garden during construction and in its spring bloom.

THE ART OF LIVING

Every fall, winter and spring for more than half a century, Medway has hosted a seasonal migration of visitors. Golfing friends arrive in November and by Thanksgiving the hunters have settled in. Christmas brings together a mixture of family and close friends, for whom the traditional singing of spirituals by the Gourdines and other African-American families at Medway is a highlight.

The New Year's Eve costume parties drew guests from all over the country and were legendary for their elaborate themes and decorations. The annual party took place in the "Log Cabin," built in 1956 to house trophies from the Legendres' hunting expeditions. Mrs. Kenyon Boocock of New York City attended New Year's parties at Medway for 40 years. "One year, the theme was a circus and Gertie arrived on the back of a baby elephant," she recalls. "Another year was a Wild West party, and Gertie, on a dare, wore her costume for the next day's dove shoot. A game warden drove up and almost arrested her." In search of costumes, Charleston friends remember going down to the Dock Street Theater and emptying Director Emmett Robinson's costume room for the party.

"New Year's Eve was not hit or miss," "Doogie" Boocock explains. "We were serious about decorating–painting backdrops and the like–and serious about costumes. The weather was always horrible, but people made the long drive anyhow. I don't remember any casualties, just a lot of fun." And always at midnight, Gertrude stepped outside to fire

*Blessed are they who to
this refuge hasten
For rest and peace to
bodies and to minds o'er
Wrought with care,
And find in it a solace,
and its soothing influence
A benediction rare.*

Lydia Child Ball,
from a poem entitled
"Medway"

her Purdey—one barrel to blow out the old year and a second to welcome in the new.

Guests at Medway usually arrive on Sunday and stay at least a week, sometimes longer. By March and April, the golfers return, joined by tennis and gardening friends. Easter brings the annual egg hunt, when 20 dozen eggs are dyed and hidden in the gardens to be discovered by the Legendre great-grandchildren, their friends and children of the staff. Gertrude's birthday at the end of March usually coincides with the blooming of the cherry trees in Grandmother's Garden.

Fresh flowers, Chinese export ware porcelains and silver candelabra are used for formal setting in the dining room.

Longtime friend and fellow conservationist George "Frolic" Weymouth drives handsome pairs of matched horses for Coaching Day, held on the Medway grounds to raise funds for Lowcountry charities.

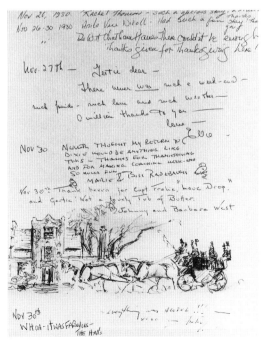

Hundreds of guests have left their mark in the Medway guest books, some more fanciful than others.

As the heat builds up in early summer, Gertrude flees Medway for the cooler climes of Fishers Island, New York. "Sidney was always reluctant to leave," Gertrude recalls, "but I could never bear the Charleston summers." Sadly, Sidney enjoyed no more than 18 years on the plantation before he suffered a heart attack in 1948.

Only 47 when he died, Sidney preferred the woods and fields to Medway's social whirl, but he could be thoroughly charming when the occasion demanded. He possessed a keen eye for detail and a clever sense of humor–as captured in the following diary entry, a rather wry appraisal of Medway's social scene in 1940:

The spring season is the open season on plantation owners for anyone that has a car and is tired of the big cities, or who does not want to motor to the North from Florida without breaking the trip en route. One of the party always knows you and they descend like locusts eating all the thoughts out of your mind leaving only the husk, an empty shell that for days can not have an original idea but only repeats what it has heard. It leaves me tired with a frustrated feeling so well wrapped up in cigarette smoke and the sight of dirty glasses that I can never quite lay my finger on just what it is that I dislike about it. The people are always amusing, polite, generally interesting if steered away from gossip, and they are flattering in their admiration of the place. Perhaps one is born sociable as you are born musical. Without this inheritance you may strive all your life and never attain the true feeling and appreciation of the genius born to his trade.

Some of the Legendres' guests over the years included Field Marshall Sir John Dill and Lady Nancy Dill in 1943, and in 1946, the British Viceroy to India, Lord Halifax and Lady Halifax must have gotten a good dose of the Lowcountry's January rains. In his thank-you note to Gertrude, he wrote: "I feel sure that if you had not sent your station wagon

Bing Crosby and his wife Kathryn visited Medway in 1965.

to meet us at the end of the dirt road, we should still be bogged down; it was so kind of you to send it."

Phillip Barry, author of *The Philadelphia Story*, and his wife Ellen, a painter, also stayed with the Legendres at Medway, as well as actors Robert Montgomery and Bing Crosby. After he and his wife, Kathryn, visited in 1965, Bing wrote: "Dear Gertie—only a wonderful person like you deserves this wonderful place." During that time, Jim Fowler of NBC's *Wild Kingdom* would also visit, bringing with him exotic animals from his travels overseas.

Another close friend was Toni Frissell, the daring fashion, portrait and sports photographer, whose

Frequent visitors included Gertie's former Foxcroft headmistress, "Miss Charlotte" Noland.

photographs of the plantation and the Lowcountry appeared in various magazines and in a book of her work. Alfred Eisenstaedt, whose publisher Henry Luce owned Mepkin Plantation on the Cooper River, photographed a deer hunt at Medway for *Life* magazine in 1938. The article was entitled "*Life* Goes to a Party: with the Sidney Legendres on a deer hunt in South Carolina."

Katherine Legendre Biddle, Sidney's sister, visited often with her husband Charles Biddle, who owned the beautiful house Andalusia, outside of Philadelphia. Nancy Lancaster, a classmate of Gertrude's at Foxcroft, was also a frequent visitor and wrote about Medway: "Gertie has made this the 'last stand' for fun, beauty and welcoming hospitality—everything!" More recently, Anne Legendre Armstrong, Sidney's niece and former presidential counselor and Ambassador to Great Britain, has been a regular guest with her husband, Texas cattleman Tobin Armstrong.

Why is it, as *Town and Country* queried in 1995, "everyone" who visits Charleston manages to find his way to Medway? Most agree the answer lies with Medway's unconventional and indomitable hostess. Dubbed an "American original," Gertrude is described by an admirer thus: "Gertie is a very lovable, remarkable lady who has given love and pleasure to so many lives, from the very famous to the simplest worker on her plantation. She is the definition of a real aristocrat, without a snobbish bone in her body."

Daughters Landine (left) and Bokara in their teens, accompanied by the ever-present Medway dogs.

Gertrude elaborates on her style of life: "I like a place to be comfortable. I'm not the formal type. I don't want to worry about where the dogs sit. A house is meant to be lived in, not toured like a museum." And this feeling of home is nowhere more evident than in the main house, which Gertrude describes as "more like an English country home—a warren of small bedrooms upstairs and a few modest sitting rooms below; cozy, warm and familiar, with fireplaces and simple wood mantles."

Medway's furnishings and decorations feel familiar as well. There are numerous inherited pieces, an

The low ceilings in the library reflect the earliest construction in the main house.

Artists working at Medway over the years included famed photographer Toni Frissell, seen here capturing preparations for a quail shoot.

extensive library, many family portraits and photographs, and other fine furniture and artwork that Gertrude has collected over the years. Her collection includes portraits by Jeremiah Theus, John Singer Sargent, Sir William Orpen and Simon Elwes. There are also artifacts, souvenirs, sculpture and ceramics from her world travels. Gertrude's personality and taste are reflected throughout.

"Not since my grandparents' day did these places feel like home and operate like plantations as Medway does today," comments writer Carola Kittredge, granddaughter of Ben Kittredge of Dean

Hall. "So many of them became syndicates after World War II, more business than home." Carola believes that Medway's long and continuing relationship with the Gourdine family contributes to this feeling. The Gourdines are a living bridge between the past and the present.

Four Gourdine family members still work on the plantation today–brothers Sam and Sirus Washington, whose mother Maggie Gourdine was born at Medway; Bertha Mae Smalls, who grew up on the plantation and is the daughter of Maggie's sister Elizabeth ("Lizzie") Gourdine; and Barbara Baylock, Bertha Mae's niece and granddaughter of Lizzie. They are part of a 25-person staff who maintain and operate the plantation. Seven staffpersons attend to the house alone–two in the pantry, three in housekeeping and two in the kitchen. Among the three guest cottages and the house, there are 14 guest beds that stay full from November to May.

Cook Christine Lofton describes Medway's style as "a little bit of country and a little bit of city."

Left:
The craftsmanship of 18th century America is seen in the finely carved cypress paneling.

Right:
Extensive travel and exploration is documented on the library walls.

Meals are prepared in the house kitchen, which has recently been remodeled. All that remains from the early days is a huge, 5-door G.E. refrigerator that looks more like something out of a morgue than a kitchen. "It holds a lot of food," says Christine.

"I can't remember but one time we used a caterer," recalls Doris Walters, Gertrude's secretary for over 30 years. "And even then, we could have done it. In 1980, we fed 300 people to celebrate Mrs. Legendre's 50th year at Medway. We started a couple of days ahead."

Preparation, especially shopping, is a bit easier now than it was in the old days. Gertrude remembers driving a mule and wagon (a car was often useless on the dirt roads) to the Mt. Holly station once a week to meet the afternoon train from Charleston that was carrying her grocery order. Many of her guests also arrived by train. Mt. Holly was a "flag stop," meaning the train wouldn't ordinarily stop there unless flagged down. The old station building stood along the tracks, not far from where the Medway Road meets Highway 52.

In the fall and winter, plantation managers and staff have for decades kept the freezer full of doves, ducks, quail and venison. Alva Johansson, who served as Gertrude's executive housekeeper from 1963 to 1990, remembers one year when there were 11 deer frozen in the cellar. Come spring, the house and table are brimming with fresh flowers and vegetables from the garden.

Winnifred McKeever, a winter resident at Yeamans Hall whose husband, Van, knew the Legendre brothers at Princeton, describes the "niceties at Medway that are all part of a bygone era"–breakfast trays every morning for the ladies, high tea in the afternoon with a magnificent silver service, candle shades on the dining-room table, finger bowls at supper and after-dinner coffee in the living room.

Lest one get the impression that life is overly formal at Medway, Marie Snowden of New York City relishes her memories of dining outside. "Whenever possible, Gertie would move us out on the terrace," she remembers. "And how we loved the luncheons in the field after dove shooting, napping on zebra skins in the grass, warmed by winter's midday sun."

As time passed, the Legendres would apply their prominent social standing and resources to philanthropic endeavors as well. One such endeavor was the construction of the Promised Land School in the 1940s for the black children of the nearby community of Strawberry. The school hall next door to the Promised Land Church had burned, so the Legendres built a new, two-room school house for the community on their Spring Grove plantation, not far from the church.

Gertrude consulted her friend and former headmistress, Charlotte Noland, founder of Foxcroft School. "Miss Charlotte" wrote back in 1941: "I have found in my long life that nothing makes one love a place more than being a constructive part of it, and if you can give those colored people 'a leg up' and get them trained for some future job, you are doing

Informal dining under the oaks or on the terrace of the Log Cabin is a long-standing Medway tradition.

Trophies from the Legendres' big-game hunts line the Log Cabin wall.

Painting window frames blue is a popular tradition in rural Carolina, as it is believed to keep bad spirits away.

something real for your South Carolina and something that will make Medway a real part of your life."

Soon after the Japanese bombed Pearl Harbor, Sidney joined the Navy as a lieutenant and Gertrude served in the Red Cross Motor Corps in Charleston. Later, she worked at the cable desk of the Office of Strategic Services (OSS), predecessor to the CIA. They left Medway in the care of their friend Henry Lowndes, who had grown up hunting at the Liberty Hall Club nearby.

On returning to Medway after World War II, Sidney and Gertrude, together with William Bennett, a retired economic consultant and winter resident at Yeamans Hall, founded the Medway Plan. They established the foundation to aid Europe after the war. Its first project was the adoption by the City of Charleston of the French town of Fleurs de l'Orne. Subsequently, 304 foreign towns were adopted by other American cities and nearly 4,000 refugees resettled.

Gertrude's longtime interest in the arts inspired the Medway Art Festival in 1958 to help raise funds for the Carolina Art Association/Gibbes Museum of

Art in Charleston. Later, she exhibited her own oil paintings and donated the proceeds to a wildlife campaign to save the snow leopard. Eventually, "Mozart at Medway" was conceived—a music festival to benefit the Charleston Symphony Orchestra.

Over the years, artists regularly set up temporary residence at Medway and availed themselves of the studio on the grounds. Inspired by Gertrude's desire to see Medway through the eyes and experiences of others, English painter Julian Barrows painted numerous scenes of the plantation and described it as an "artist's paradise." Other friends and painters, such as Charles Baskerville, Simon Elwes, A. Lassell Ripley, John Henry Dick and Frolic Weymouth, came as well. Charleston artist Alfred Hutty, whose well-known etchings of live oaks were largely inspired by the trees at nearby Yeamans Hall Plantation, gave Gertrude a painting lesson at Medway. Several of his paintings and prints, as well as his wax sculpture of potato pickers, are displayed on the second floor of the main house.

Today, cabinetmaker Bob Walbaum works at Medway. Bob has worked for ten years on the plantation, attending to "all that concerns wood," from fencing to fine furniture. He often works with woods such as walnut, cypress and longleaf pine, harvested directly from the plantation. "I hope to be involved with Medway for the rest of my life," Bob says.

Artist Tony Henneberg also spent several winters at Medway, painting wildlife and portraits. His passion is birds, which he has painted since the age of five. Tony informally tutored Gertrude and a group of her friends and local artists, who came to Medway periodically for painting sessions on the grounds.

Medway's artistic legacy actually reaches back to the Stoney era at the turn of the century, when artists and writers frequented the plantation. Louisa Stoney was a charter member of The Poetry Society of

South Carolina and cultivated friendships with DuBose Heyward, John Bennett, Josephine Pinckney, Yates Snowden and Hervey Allen, all of whom visited Medway and were leaders in the "Charleston Renaissance." Inspiring works of literature and art came from this period, including *The Carolina Low-Country,* a popular book whose dust jacket is graced by a colored woodblock print of Medway by artist Anna Heyward Taylor.

For those seeking artistic inspiration or simply a respite from city life, Medway serves up a nourishing blend of beauty, comfort and peace. Horace ("Ho") Kelland, a friend and artist who met Gertrude at Fishers Island one summer in the '50s, readily accounts for the lure of Medway: "Everywhere I travel, when I mention to an acquaintance that I spend the winters in Charleston, immediately they ask, 'Have you been to Medway?' It is a place that is known far and wide, a place so full of fun and inspiration. Without Gertie and Medway, we would all be much poorer."

New York artist Charles Baskerville chose Medway as the subject of his well-known landscape paintings.

The Natural Environment

A Portfolio of Photographs
by
Thomas Blagden, Jr.

Crane Pond, water lily pads and marsh

Floating bladderwort and water lily pads

Dawn on David's Pond

Freshwater marsh with autumn cypress

Pied-billed grebe

Great blue heron

Woodcock

Purple gallinule

Ring-necked duck

American alligator

Wood duck

Great egret

Bluebird

Common gallinule

Fledgling red-shouldered hawk

Water lily and baby alligator

Back River, pickerelweed, cattails and water primrose

Autumn cypress trees

Rose vine, Home Reserve

Chinese tallow leaves and moss

THE BROTHERHOOD
OF NIMROD

After the Civil War, southern planters forged a new relationship with their plantations. In a sense, they rediscovered the untamed landscape of their colonial ancestors. From the once ordered and profitable fields and tidelands, they shifted to the wild interiors and gamelands. Having been stripped of their agricultural wealth by an invading army, plantation owners invested themselves, economically and emotionally, in one of their few remaining assets, the hunting grounds. As planters gave way to hunters and sportsmen, they in turn evolved into conservationists.

Captain Sam Stoney (1853-1926) came of age during the turmoil of Reconstruction. Inspired by Sir Walter Scott's *Ivanhoe*, he competed in ring tournaments, and pursued wild game at Medway with the zeal of an Old Testament warrior. He relished the ritualistic nature of the hunt, initiating first-time deer slayers into what he called "The Brotherhood of Nimrod," carrying on the tradition of painting an initiate's face, neck and hair with the blood of his kill.

When Captain Stoney was 22 years old, he formed a hunt club with his Uncle Peter, owner of Medway, called "The Goslings." Using large packs of hounds managed by "drivers" (usually black huntsmen), the uncle and nephew along with other former planters pursued deer through the woods on horseback. The mounted deer drive had been practiced on Lowcountry plantations for generations. Often hunters fired from horseback, which required a great deal of skill. They likened their sport to that of fox hunting in England and followed a prescribed social code. The Medway Hunt Book contains a description of Laurence O'Hear in pursuit of a buck on January 2, 1876:

...the buck turned and ran back through the drive followed by the whole pack....he [Mr. O'Hear] *skirted around the edge of the drive to meet the dogs at a point when the deer usually ran out; this point was on the Back River Road, and as soon as he reached the road, he put his horse out to full speed, and had run about two hundred*

Sidney Legendre in shooting attire.

yards, when his horse struck some object, which was darting across the road; the horse rolled completely over, throwing O'Hear some distance in front of him; in looking after his fall, what was his astonishment to see a deer struggling, under his horse; the horse soon regained his legs and the deer dragged itself a short distance from the road, where the dogs caught it a few minutes later....After carrying the deer home and skinning it, it was examined carefully and the only mark of injury found was on the skin where the hoof of the horse had evidently struck it.

For many southerners deer was the most prized quarry of all. By 1750, elk and bison had disappeared from Carolina, and deer had become the most important species of game for food and hides. According to museum curator Christopher Boyle, "records show that Charles Town exported an average of 54,000 skins annually between 1699 and 1715." Deerskin hats, coats and gloves were the rage in Europe. By the early 19th century, some localities of extensive agricultural lands were already barren of deer. However, where the woods, swamps and thickets still prevailed, such as at Medway, the deer flourished. (Marks, 1991) The thrill and comradeship of the chase over vast acreage of woodland made deer hunting the preferred sport for plantation owners like the Stoneys.

In 1906, Captain Stoney purchased Medway from his uncle's family and established the Back River Hunting Club. His wife, Louisa Stoney, wrote in *A Day on Cooper River* that Medway, along with Pine Grove to the north, and Parnassus, Brick Hope and Liberty Hall Plantations to the south, "were enclosed...in one park fence and in-season deer were hunted twice a week from one of the 5 houses."

The hunting rules for "Medway Park" reveal the origin of Medway's "hall of horns," so often noted by visitors: "All heads of horns procured in the park are to be placed on the walls of the Hall of Medway

And Cush begat Nimrod: he began to be a mighty one in the earth. He was a mighty hunter before the Lord: wherefore it is said, Even as Nimrod the mighty hunter before the Lord.

Genesis 10:8-9

House, and duly inscribed with the name of hunter and date of hunt." As one guest wrote the Captain in 1919: "I know of no pleasure that would equal that of sitting under the antlers of those bucks...adorning the walls at 'Medway,' and listening to the stories and the many hunts that have taken place there."

A hunting party would typically arrive at Medway in the morning by train, boat, horseback or, later, by automobile. An assortment of saddled horses usually awaited them, some belonging to Captain Stoney, others borrowed or rented from neighbors and black huntsmen. The pack of hounds numbered anywhere from five to twenty dogs, and were of varied origin.

A hunt would often begin at Pine Grove and follow drives across Medway and over to Parnassus and "The Cottage," where the party would take lunch. The hunters would resume driving deer in the afternoon and by evening they worked their way back to Medway, carrying their slain deer in a wagon. It might be 11 p.m. before they finished skinning and butchering the venison, hanging it from a tree by the light of a fire.

Each drive or section had a name, such as Marshfield, Shallow Branch, Broom Grass, Prioleau Branch or Bachman's Bay. These areas were preferred because they contained some of the southern whitetail deer's favorite hiding places. The popular outdoor writer Archibald Rutledge, who hunted with Captain Stoney at Medway, described these hiding places for *Field and Stream* in 1915: "At night they feed and roam about. Toward dawn...they will either go into 'branches' (densely grown ponds and water-courses that intersect the pineland at frequent intervals), or else they will lie down in the broom-grass in some remote part of the woods....In such a retreat, if well-hidden, a deer will often count on being passed by, and will occasionally permit a

hunter to ride or walk almost within touching distance."

On a Thanksgiving hunt in 1911, the sixth and
final drive was particularly memorable: "Seven deer
were jumped in this drive, at intervals of ten to fifteen
minutes in groups of two and three. The dogs scattered as well as the drivers and the shooting, excited
warnings of the drivers, and the cry of the divided
pack made this the most exciting drive of the hunt."

Women occasionally accompanied the men and,

*Gertie, flanked by her
brother Laddie (l.) and
brother-in-law Morris
Legendre (r.), with houseman Sam Broughton and
friends inspecting a suc-
cessful "morning bag."*

in 1915, the Medway Hunt Book records a description of what the writer terms "a small hunt [that] was organized to give the ladies a shot." The passage suggests how hunting often reflected the prevailing social hierarchy of the sexes: "An accommodating deer, a buck, was jumped on this occasion which was gloriously missed by 'Mass Pushay.' A vision then appeared to Miss D. Salley of a hornless deer running toward Mr. Hyde; she states upon oath that the sweetness of its expression was such that no one could have shot at it and besides she did not believe that blood became her complexion....Never did Acteon meet with a more tenderhearted Diana."

The writer continues: "The buck—which it now appeared to be, next passed Miss Emma Rutledge who missed it with a great deal of skill, calling on the name of her Maker, in a most pious fashion, all the while. Miss Maybank and Miss Stoney [Captain Stoney's daughter Harriet] on the next stand now fired and fell back. Though owing to the fact that her safety catch was on when she [Harriet] first started into action, it was wonderful that she shot at all. Miss Maybank, the innocent bystander, says the deer and the gun went off at the same time."

Attitudes toward female hunters were changing, however. In 1917, Archibald Rutledge wrote to Captain Stoney: "On Dec. 26th, Mrs. Frank Ford of Summerville killed two deer at one shot. It is high time for men to take a back seat." Another friend wrote of his wife in 1921: "...Rachel is not only as good a shot as Adams and myself, but I am going to see if she cannot do just as well as Captain Samuel G. Stoney." In fact, Capt. Stoney's own daughter Harriet was a skilled horsewoman and on her birthday was presented with a 20-gauge shotgun from her godfather.

Critical to the success of a deer hunt were the drivers. The most revered of Medway's drivers during the Stoney era was David Gourdine, Sr., usually referred to as "Davy" in the hunting accounts. David was born at Medway, and was probably descended from the slave Dublin Gourdin(e), whose name occurs frequently in an 1872 plantation account book and whose death was the subject of a poem written by Louisa Stoney. Dublin's family adopted the last name of Gourdin(e), a 17th century French Huguenot name belonging to several Cooper River plantation owners. Dublin's family chose one of the oldest surnames found in the Lowcountry. (Steen, 1996)

John James Audubon and William Elliott (author of the popular 19th century book *Carolina Sports by Land and Water...*) referred to deer drivers in their writings; the position was more highly regarded in the hierarchy of plantation life than that of many slaves or workers. In fact, the position of the African-American deer driver continued long after the Civil War, and became a link between the past and the present for both black and white. The driver was in charge of the horses and the hounds, often taking part in the training of both. He commanded the dogs either by voice or the crack of a whip. The position demanded skill in horsemanship and a thorough knowledge of the hunting grounds and habits of the game.

Deer drivers such as David Gourdine possessed great stamina as well. Medway deer hunts often ran five, six or even seven drives in one day, each drive lasting between one and one-and-a-half hours. The January chases could be bitterly cold, as was one New Year's Day hunt in 1918: There was "severe cold, the ground—being covered with snow, and everything frozen up....Two deer ran to Mr. S. G. Gaillard who fired both barrels wounding a small buck, which was afterwards caught on the ice at Toomer's reserve [just below Medway house and now called 'Home Reserve']. The ice was so thick

David Gourdine, Jr. and Cy Myers, skilled drivers and hunters whose families have lived and worked at Medway for more than a hundred years.

that Davy was able to push the boat on the ice and get the deer without even cracking the ice."

David's daughter Lizzie Gourdine, who lived and worked at Medway for over fifty years, remembers her father's death on September 13th, 1921: "It was a Saturday morning and he was on his way to hunt. He was mounting his horse by the [Medway] house and he staggered back twice. Mr. Stoney grabbed him from the back and laid him there on the well. Then Mr. Stoney burned the end of a hat pin and stuck my father in the left side; there was no feeling. They thought it must have been a stroke. They took him to the city [Charleston], to Roper Hospital, and Tuesday morning Mr. Stoney came to our house to break the news that my father had died."

On hearing of David's death, many of Captain Stoney's friends wrote to express their sadness: "I was grieved to hear of the death of Davy," wrote Alexander Taylor. "He was a born hunter and his true and keen appreciation of the sport, his skill in driving, together with his inexhaustible fund of rich anecdotes will make us miss him sadly this Christmas...." David was buried in his family's graveyard at Medway and the Stoneys placed a gravestone there, inscribed with the following epitaph:

> *A keen Sportsman and*
> *famous Deer Driver*
> *No more his mellow horn*
> *shall sound*
> *His echoing voice rouse*
> *flagging hound.*

David's sons, David Jr. (1895-1961) and Walter Gourdine (1905-1978), followed in their father's footsteps, residing at Medway and becoming skilled drivers, horsemen, hunters and trappers. They too are buried on the plantation with their father. David's grandson Sam Washington continues the Gourdine legacy. His story connects Medway's past with the present.

Sam was born on Christmas Day in 1949 and spent his boyhood farming, hunting and fishing. He and his ten brothers and sisters grew up in a four-room, frame house with no plumbing or electricity. The family cooked and warmed themselves by a wood stove, lit their cabin with kerosene lanterns and drank from a freshwater spring. For a while, Sam and his brothers attended the Promised Land School built by the Legendres. Later, Sam graduated from Berkeley High School.

"We had no refrigerator or freezer," Sam remembers, "so we would cut and dry deer meat by the fire. We also hunted squirrel, beaver, and even alligator for the tail meat. We fished for mullet, brim and bass in the Black [Back] River. We would walk from one plantation to another, for miles, looking for good banks to fish from."

As a young man, Sam helped with hunts at neighboring Bluff Plantation and undertook various jobs at Medway. Today, he works as Gertrude Legendre's chief houseman and chauffeur, and on the weekends in season, drives deer for a hunt club at Millbrook Plantation on the Ashley River. His life has revolved around Medway and the surrounding woods and waters, and he is passionate about preserving them.

Today, only a handful of South Carolina planta-

Walter Gourdine followed in his father's footsteps as one of the Lowcountry's famed horsemen and trappers.

tions still practice the mounted deer drive, with only a handful of black huntsmen, like Sam Washington, still working as drivers. Those who carry on the "Brotherhood of Nimrod" do so for many of the same reasons that compelled Captain Stoney a century earlier—the comradeship, the thrill of the chase and the connection to nature and the past.

David Gourdine, Jr. with two foxes.

WING SHOOTING

Though the excitement of a deer chase more readily stirred his passions, Captain Stoney also pursued quail. He recorded a relative abundance of them at Medway in 1909. That year, he devoted his Christmas hunt to bird shooting and reported that "eight coveys were found and a good bag brought in" over the course of the morning. On another day, four coveys were found in one hour within a mile of the house, as well as some woodcock, one within a few feet of the front piazza.

That same year, William Read wrote to his "Cousin Sam" from Philadelphia: "I wish you would tell 'Davie'...that we want him to keep those turkeys well fed....I notice he reports deer abundant and it certainly makes me wild to get once again among the plentiful game on your place. The thought of finding thirteen coveys of quail in five hours, such as you did, makes one's mouth water...."

Indeed, the tender meat of the quail was considered a delicacy, as William Elliott described in *Carolina Sports by Land and Water:* "...it should be eaten with none but champagne sauce, and in no posture but on one's knees–through thankfulness." The little bobwhite came to represent the nobility of the animal world; and those who hunted them, the aristocrats of hunters. For many, wild quail lands, which were abundant in the Lowcountry, were the most coveted hunting grounds of all.

Scholar Stuart Marks writes in his book *Southern Hunting in Black and White:* "Quail are the stuff of Southern traditions. The pursuit of quail is linked in the myth of the Southern gentleman whose land ownership is his source of wealth, prestige, and independence. The fidelity of quail to place (small home range), their response to habitat improvements and to stewardship (favorite coveys shot year after year), their pursuit with special breeds of dogs (pointers and setters) that 'honor' each other's points...their sudden bursts into flight (separates cool sportsmen from their pretenders), and their cockiness and pronouncements of presence (they whistle their own names!) are some of the characteristics seized upon to construct durable structures of emotion and ritual. The irony is that the prestige of quail hunting is of recent vintage and one in which Yankee wealth played a large, creative role."

Where else in the eastern United States was there sufficient woodland acreage left to support free-roaming large mammals and wild fowl? Without a doubt, the South had cornered the market on wild gamelands, and as a result, plantation owners gained new status in the sporting field. The railroads capitalized on the growing popularity of hunting by providing the essential link between northern cities and southern hunting grounds. They circulated pamphlets to lure sportsmen "to visit the South and hunt game where it is more plentiful than in any other section of the United States." (Leffingwell, 1895)

Certainly for Gertrude and Sidney Legendre, the presence of abundant wild game at Medway was especially alluring, as was the sense of adventure found in the southern "wilderness" of the early 20th century. No doubt they sensed certain similarities between the Carolina Lowcountry and the hunting grounds of Africa and Asia they so eagerly explored. Travel and communications were difficult and slow. Extensive gamelands harbored abundant wildlife—with wildcats and bears roaming the forests, and alligators and snakes plying the swamps. Even native

Opposite:
Abundant game and mild winters made hunting one of the principal activities of the plantation.

palm trees thrived in the semitropical climate.

After they purchased Medway from the Stoneys in 1929, the Legendres hosted season after season of hunters, many of whom would arrive by train at the Mount Holly station, just four miles from Medway's door. The hunts were held six days a week and were as much social as they were sport. Noted wildlife scholars and conservationists who hunted at Medway included Dillon Ripley, Kurt Wentzel, Erard Matthiessen, John Henry Dick, Alexander Sprunt, Milby Burton and, of course, Archibald Rutledge.

Like many northern and southern sportsmen, the Legendres preferred quail to deer. In 1939, Sidney reported 162 bobwhite shot at Medway in just two weeks. One December day, ten coveys were flushed in less than two hours. In his diary, Sidney described

Carola (foreground) and Ben Kittredge of Dean Hall, who introduced the Legendres to Medway.

setting out on a quail shoot: "We were to shoot in the morning, Gertrude, Ben Kittredge and myself. Carola Kittredge and Audrey [Emery]…rode in a buggy….Little David [David Gourdine, Jr.] had the quail wagon bursting with bird dogs. With him rode Walter [David's brother], whose job it was to jump off and seize our horses' heads when we dismounted to shoot. Jimmy Becker and Millie were also on horses and we looked like a regiment leaving the house."

They hunted over seven large sections or units of Medway's approximately 7,000 acres, riding in mule-drawn buckboards or astride Lowcountry ponies called "marsh tackies," which were better adapted to the South Carolina climate than thoroughbreds. The dogs, usually English setters, and their handler were critical to locating the quail. Once the dogs were "on point," two designated shooters would dismount quickly, move in and prepare to fire, side by side. Gertrude preferred English double-barrel shotguns, either an Evans or a Purdey.

"It was a safe hunt, a cordial shoot," remembers Gertrude. "We did not overhunt the coveys and allowed only three or four birds to be taken from each. The dogs were always under control, and we seldom went after single birds."

Turkeys and doves were also plentiful on Medway. On an October day in 1935, 42 turkeys were seen. One January, 240 doves were shot in one day. Dove shoots tended to be social in nature and were often accompanied by luncheon in the field. Sidney described such an occasion in December of 1940:

Luncheon was laid under the pines and tables covered with yellow cloths and set with crude pottery plates….Everyone was seated and then sherry was passed….Gertrude had ordered a marvelous meal. Hot bean soup, chicken mushrooms and rice all mixed together. Sweet potato pie with marshmallows on top, and succotash.

Sam [Broughton] *passed a heaping plate full of corn bread sticks in one hand and beer in the other. And then to end, we had apple pie and cheese, finished with coffee....*

Hardly had the guns taken their stands that the doves began to come in. Sometimes they would come singly and sometimes in flocks of ten or more. Though they flew well and the sixteen guns shot one hundred and twenty birds, it was nothing like the old days when they poured into the same field in the hundreds and one's gun was hot, unbearably so, and one's shoulder tired so that the ending horn was welcomed.

Ducks also took refuge at Medway. Gertrude recalls that in the 1930s, Medway hosted some 25,000 waterfowl each winter on the many ponds or impoundments scattered about the plantation. One of the oldest wintering grounds at Medway is Crane Pond, originally an inland swamp that was impounded as a freshwater rice reserve in the 1700s. Each year the 60-acre pond harbors between four and five thousand ring-necked ducks, "buzzing like bees," as one guest described in 1956. When duck populations began to decline nationwide, the Legendres declared Crane Pond a refuge and limited duck shooting to no more than two or three hunts a year, usually at holidays.

Sidney described duck hunting at Medway on a cold morning in 1940:

Slowly the blackness turned to gray. Low dark clouds were scudding across the sky that pressed down on the marsh driving the ducks into low skimming flights. The water lapped against the side of the boat as the negro paddled, and occasionally there was the faint swish of grass, the tall yellow marsh grass rubbing against our sides. Overturned lily pads and ducks were indistinguishable in the half real light and only the whir of wings coming out of the darkness with a screech like ripping cloth told us that the birds were already on the wing.

My blind lay on the edge of a growth of marsh grass. As

Carefully organized hunts contributed to Medway's reputation as one of the south's premier wildlife management plantations. (l.-r.) David Gourdine, Jr., Mary Sanford, Jane Sanford Pansa, and Laddie Sanford.

I stood on the platform the sides reached to my shoulders giving me freedom to swing my gun. The negro threw the old faded decoys into the water, and they landed with a tired splash as if this existence was well known and they were thoroughly bored with it.

The ducks came in great waves like an attacking army. There were some that dove down onto the decoys like Stukas. Others drifted down with set wings as calmly and smoothly as a commercial air liner making a landing. Then as I arose from the obscurity of the blind they drew their feet in and flaying the air with their wings attempted to climb from the sudden danger that arose before them. Occasionally flocks of blue wing teal swept by low and unseen until too late.

*And above my head, high above my head, floated great
mallards with craning necks examining every blade of grass,
peering at each open body of water with the eyes of the perpetual unbeliever. No wooden decoys can fool them; no
blind so hidden that they cannot see one. Yet at times they
lose their caution and will drop down with outspread
wings onto a gunner so exposed that even a ring neck would
avoid him.*

As Sidney's journal indicates, it was neither the
lovely house, nor the gardens nor the social life that
had the most profound effect on the young couple,
but rather the old hunting grounds. As they searched
for game in Medway's fields and forests, their daily

encounters with both the beautiful and precarious sides of nature deepened Gertrude and Sidney's relationship to the plantation. The damp chill of a spring morning; the faint, sharp smell of freshly cut logs; the sight of a bald eagle hovering over a nervous flock of ducks; the hoot of an owl in the cold darkness of winter—the basic, physical forces of the landscape would leave an indelible mark on the Legendres, just as they had on the Stoneys.

Sidney Legendre (opposite) *and Gertie* (right) *prepare for quail shooting on horseback.*

AN ENDANGERED HABITAT

More than 50 years passed as southern and northern hunters explored the Carolina "wilderness," recasting their relationship with nature and their role in society. No longer were they primarily engaged in ordering the landscape. The challenge became one of understanding and knowing the ways of nature in order to reap its bounty, both physical and spiritual. Nature and man were coming together in a new, postagrarian relationship.

A community was developing around the southern plantations out of which a modern conservation ethic would emerge. In 1846, William Elliott sowed the seeds of such an ethic in his conclusion to *Carolina Sports By Land and Water...*: "...we may yet hope to see the time when men may, under the sanction of the law, and without offence, or imputation of aristocracy, preserve the game from extermination—and perpetuate, in so doing, the healthful, generous, and noble diversion of hunting." Some 60 years later, in 1909, the Medway Hunt Book records a meeting between the Stoneys and James Henry Rice Jr., secretary of the Audubon Society: "...we discussed the game laws fully and the necessity for the passage of the 'License Law' which would be of the greatest benefit to our efforts at Game Protection."

By 1909, the Charleston Natural History Society (now a chapter of the National Audubon Society) was leading field trips to Medway. Such groups had begun to focus on nongame species of wildlife and appreciated the value of plantation gamelands and rice reserves for their survival. Of course, elk and bison had long ago disappeared from the Lowcountry and by the turn of the century, the large predatory mammals—panthers, wolves and bears—were scarce. Avian species such as the passenger pigeon, ivory-billed woodpecker and Carolina parakeet hovered near extinction. The decline of these animals was largely attributed to extensive agricultural clearing, overhunting and excessive timbering of the native pine forests and cypress swamps.

The cypress swamps along the Cooper and Back Rivers were highly prized in the 17th, 18th and 19th centuries, particularly for their timber and freshwater supply. At the same time, it was believed the wild, uncultivated swamp harbored bad airs (malaria), frightening beasts and evil spirits. Nevertheless, colonial artists and naturalists such as Mark Catesby extolled the virtues of these areas as great reservoirs of natural beauty. Today, "an alarming number of the animals and plants identified by these writers and artists—strange and exciting species that had essentially signified America to Europe—are now endangered or extinct." (Beach, 1992)

Medway's 389 acres of hardwood and cypress swamp follow the watershed of Back River and intersect the upland pine forests at various intervals. They harbor thousands of wood ducks year round, a duck so beautifully arrayed that its Latin name, "sponsa," means "chosen one" or "bride." In spring, migrating songbirds, such as the prothonotary warbler, arrive from South America. The prothonotary nests in the holes and cavities of cypress "knees" and feeds on insects. Families of alligators breed in the swamps as well, the yellow-striped young carefully guarded by their mothers. Wild atamasco lilies, called "naked ladies," grow at the water's edge, near where purple gallinules and little blue herons feed.

Medway's other endangered habitat, the longleaf

pine forest—where Captain Stoney chased deer on horseback and the Legendres pursued quail—once dominated Carolina's upland coastal plain. Called the "Great Savanna" by early mapmakers, 70 to 90 million acres of the parklike forest once blanketed the Southeast from Virginia to Texas. Here, under the widely spaced canopy of towering pines, buffalo grazed on succulent grasses, quail thrived on seed-producing legumes and deer browsed on "running oaks."

Sidney Legendre described riding on horseback through Medway's longleaf forest on a quail hunt one February morning in 1940: "The warm sun beat down shutting our eyes, coating the long grass with gold, throwing the pines onto the ground, long black lines that lay on the brown of the needles."

Today the slow-growing, dense longleaf is known as the "Cadillac" of southern pines because of its superior strength for pole and saw timber, and its ability to withstand hurricanes, fire and disease. The sunny understory contains hundreds of species of vascular plants, including bluestem, blazing star, Catesby's lily, white-fringed orchid, rayless goldenrod and carnivorous pitcher plants. The many flowering plants provide a banquet for migrating butter-

Medway's longleaf pine forest provides shelter for 16 colonies of rare and endangered red-cockaded woodpeckers.

flies. Above, pine warblers and eastern bluebirds feed among the large cones and needles found in the canopy. In fact, some 40 rare or endangered species of flora and fauna are found in South Carolina's vanishing longleaf habitat. Unfortunately, less than four million acres of longleaf forest remain in the Southeast. It has become one of the most endangered ecosystems in North America.

Medway contains about 2,500 acres of this extraordinary forest. Unlike planted pines, most of Medway's longleaf forest is genetically pure, having naturally regenerated from seeds of original stock. Longleaf grows best on the higher elevations of the plantation, whereas loblolly pine forest (some 2,300 acres) typically exists in the lower, wetter areas adjacent to the swamps of Back River. Both the endangered eastern fox squirrel and red-cockaded woodpecker prefer the open longleaf woods. In fact, Medway is home to 16 colonies of this rare woodpecker.

Like the African plains and Western prairies, longleaf habitat depends on seasonal fires. In the past, the lightning fires of spring and summer cleansed the forest floor of emergent hardwood species and made way for a myriad of herbaceous plants. Fire also pre-

Seasonal burnings of forest undergrowth are crucial to wildlife management.

pared the soil to receive the seedfall of the longleafs. Death or injury to wild animals by fire was not common. In fact, game tended to congregate on a fresh burn, prompting the Indians to use fire as a hunting tool. (Komarek, 1982)

Three large spring fires were described in the Medway Hunt Book in 1910, 1911 and 1913. These were accidental fires and considered disastrous at the time. In March of 1910, there was unusually dry weather with high winds, and a fire swept through the woods for five days: "...[the fire] had practically burned out completely an area of nearly 1800 acres: this was the most disastrous fire seen on the place since the war [Civil War]." The following spring, more fires occurred: "Serious forest fires have been raging for the past two weeks and notwithstanding the efforts of tenants and help. Coppin Race Course, Broom Grass and Prioleau Branch have been burned out."

Then in April of 1913, fire burned about 3,000 acres, through all of Medway's hunting areas. Captain Stoney wrote: "This was the most destructive and disastrous fire that has ever visited these properties...destroys the prospect of any hunting of turkey, quail....Fire started by sparks from logging locomotive of the Cooper River Corporation...all due to negligence and indifference on the part of the company logging the timber on Medway." The benefits of such a fire, however, would soon be appreciated. The Captain's nephew, Henry Smythe, remembers hearing his father, Augustine Smythe, tell of the great numbers of quail he shot at Medway the following year when he and his fiance, Harriott Buist, visited the plantation just before marrying in 1914.

Edward Komarek, a longleaf and fire ecologist who visited Medway in 1940, wrote that the southern hunting plantations played a significant role in shaping the longleaf pine forest:

"As land was periodically fallowed, particularly in the South, and the practice of burning for livestock and other purposes continued, the game populations of some of the southeastern areas must have increased tremendously during the period after the Civil War.... During this period scattered hunting plantations on old rice plantations were developed along the South Carolina coast as well as on Edisto and Hilton Head Islands.... By the early 1930s there were well over 200 hunting plantations with an average size of about 10,000 acres scattered from coastal North Carolina, around the coast and into southern Alabama and Mississippi. Essentially this development followed the range of the longleaf pine."

Sidney invited Komarek's colleague Herbert Stoddard to visit Medway in the late '30s and early '40s to assess declining quail populations. [Sidney, a member of Stoddard's Cooperative Quail Study Association, had begun to notice a gradual loss of pine forest to scrub oak. He lamented the subsequent reduction in quail numbers and possible lowering of timber value.] Stoddard, a friend of Aldo Leopold's, was known as the "father" of modern wildlife management for his pioneering quail research in Thomasville, Georgia. He concluded that many southern pine forests were suffering from suppression of fire. He advocated mimicking nature—with the use of controlled burns, minimal soil disturbance, natural regeneration and selective harvesting—to sustain a pine forest and its wildlife populations for the long-term.

It was not until the early 1950s, however, that the principles of wildlife management were applied successfully to timber production at Medway. When William (Bill) Baldwin became Medway's consulting forester and wildlife biologist in the early 1950s, Stoddard's theory was successfully applied to the plantation's timber production. Woody undergrowth

Conservation seminars led by forester Bill Baldwin pioneered efforts to adopt sound land management for the Lowcountry.

was "choking" Medway's forest, so he began to burn the woods at regular intervals to open them up again. He also harvested the forest one tree at a time. His son, author Billy Baldwin, remembers his father's technique: "He would mark the individual trees and then step back and ask 'now how does that look?' Then he would pretend to hold a rifle in his hands and swing it around to see if he could get a clear shot through the forest he was shaping...always considering the aesthetics and the quail."

Bill also enhanced Medway's duck habitat, fixing up the old waterfowl ponds and creating new ones. With a crew of workmen, he raised and repaired old ricefield dikes and installed new "trunks" or floodgates. By burning off unwanted vegetation and manipulating the water levels, Bill promoted the growth of wild plants favored by waterfowl. By the time the ducks arrived in the fall, a veritable feast awaited them on Medway's 462 acres of ricefields and ponds.

For both quail and duck, Bill focused on enhancing their particular habitats to promote the growth of their preferred natural foods. Gertrude credits Bill with bringing the birds back to Medway: "He loved nature. He trained as a wildlife biologist, then taught himself forestry. He really made this place what it is." Bill was a founding trustee of the Nature Conservancy of South Carolina and was instrumental in establishing the Francis Beidler Forest Audubon Sanctuary.

In 1978, Bill retired from Medway and Gertrude turned to a young biologist named Robert (Bob) Hortman for management. Bob apprenticed with Bill for a year and has lived at Medway ever since with his wife, Janet, and two sons. "In a sense, I am carrying on what Bill Baldwin and others before him began," comments Bob. "We are hunting the descendants of the same deer and birds that Sam Stoney and Archibald Rutledge hunted one hundred years ago," he reflects. "During a duck hunt in Crane Pond a while back, I was paddling my boat and could feel it bump against the submerged posts of an old blind that Captain Stoney probably once set. When I reached into the cold, black water to retrieve a ring-neck, I imagined I saw the reflection of the Captain handing me that bird. I hope that our children's children will reach into these same waters and wonder about the reflections from the past."

As plantation manager, Bob oversees 15 of Medway's staff in maintaining the woodlands, the impoundments, the grounds, the house and outbuildings, and over 50 miles of dirt roads. He views his life at Medway as a continuous cycle of work, family, recreation, conservation and art, all revolving around a reverence for the earth. In his precious spare time, an abiding interest in birds inspired Bob to draw, then to pursue taxidermy, and finally to carve wooden sculptures.

In 1989, Hurricane Hugo gave Bob the challenge of his life. On September 21st, in the dead of night, Hugo's 135 mile-per-hour winds felled 5,000 acres of trees, 63% of Medway's timber inventory. Doris Walters, Gertrude's secretary, remembers the storm as if it were yesterday: "I wasn't afraid till the next morning when I looked out my window. For the first time, I could see the sun rise over Back River because the forest I knew was no longer there." Logging crews eventually hauled 3,657 truckloads of fallen sawtimber off the plantation.

For six long days, Doris, Bob, and the other staff in residence were cut off entirely from the outside world while they cleared the main road leading into the plantation. Gertrude, in France at the time, rushed to Medway the following week. There was no electricity, so Bob cranked up some generators and Gertrude stayed with Doris while she and the staff assessed the damage.

Next door to Doris, Lizzie Gourdine's old house was demolished by a tremendous pine tree that fell across the roof. Fortunately, no one was living there at the time. Another fallen tree destroyed the greenhouse and wrecked the walled kitchen garden. To everyone's amazement, however, the old pink house stood unscathed, a beacon in a sea of fallen trees. Furthermore, Gertrude herself seemed undaunted by the surrounding destruction, saying over and over to her staff, "Look what's left." As Bob says, "She understood the cycle of destruction and recovery. She was seeing what we couldn't see." Indeed, the plantation recovered rapidly from Hugo's fury, but far more threatening forces were looming at Medway's borders.

SAVING THE PAST FOR THE FUTURE

After Hurricane Hugo tore through Medway in 1989, Gertrude Legendre realized that while Nature's forces were reshaping the plantation, the forces of human development threatened to eliminate it altogether. In one woman's lifetime an entire landscape was disappearing. The old hunting grounds of Parnassus and Liberty Hall had become a naval weapons station, Ben Kittredge's Dean Hall was now a chemical plant, and Mount Holly Plantation across Highway 52 was an aluminum factory. Three or four times a year, real estate brokers were calling Gertrude to ask whether she would sell Medway for development. With sardonically evocative street names like "Mossy Oak," "Evergreen Magnolia" and "Pecan Grove," commercial and residential sprawl was beginning to blight other plantation lands in the area.

Would Medway—a place whose residents participated in the birth of the American nation and the fall of the Confederacy, where tremendous engineering feats and manufacturing enterprises occurred in the name of rice and bricks, where writers and artists created works of great inspiration, where ancient forests and swamps harbored generation after generation of unique and rare species—be the next to be ruined? At Medway the history of nation as well as region had been preserved in a magnificent, biologically diverse setting.

In 1991, Gertrude acted. She decided to donate two perpetual conservation easements—one to the Historic Charleston Foundation to protect the his-

Friends tell me that I have left my mark on Medway, and I can only say that this historic property has left its mark on me.

Gertrude Sanford
Legendre

toric plantation house and the surrounding buildings and grounds (approximately 83 acres); and the other to the Ducks Unlimited Foundation to preserve nearly 6,000 acres of Medway's forests and wetlands. Word for word the crux of the easements is set forth in both prefaces: "Medway Plantation possesses significant historic, natural, archaeological, scenic, wildlife, habitat, and open space values (collectively, 'conservation values') of great importance to Grantor, to the people of South Carolina, to Grantee, and to the people of this nation...[and] Grantor intends to preserve and protect the conservation values of the Property in perpetuity."

With these easements, Gertrude gave up all development rights to Medway for herself and for successive owners. Although these easements may have decreased Medway's "market" value, the value of preserving the plantation for future generations far exceeded–to her–the loss in potential profits from development. The plantation's two miles of waterfront and adjacent swamps, along with its exquisite uplands, would be spared the ravages of the bulldozer so that traditional activities of timbering, farming, hunting and game management could continue. Public educational, charitable and research activities would also be allowed.

Such outstanding safeguards were the culmination of Gertrude's evolution from sportswoman to conservationist. She had grown up in an era when hawks and wildcats were considered "vermin" and game animals were regarded as "the ladies and gentlemen of the animal world." Yet fifty years later, Gertrude would delight in the yearly arrival of a nesting red-shouldered hawk outside her bedroom window and marvel at the prowess of a bobcat chasing down a squirrel on the lawn. Having witnessed the worldwide decimation of so many species in her lifetime, she envisaged that someday Medway might become an oasis in a desert of concrete, "what Central Park is to New York City."

Like her good friend John Henry Dick, Gertrude began to look beyond her quest for game. Tired of shooting, she hoped to provide a refuge for the animals she loved. She consulted with Peter Berle of the Audubon Society and Russell Train of World Wildlife Fund, both of whom visited Medway in the late '80s and early '90s. She concluded that conservation easements were the most permanent way possible to ensure that future generations of wildlife would find sanctuary at Medway. Gertrude states simply, "I want Medway to be a place where the beasts can grow old and die." Other plantation owners in the area have followed suit, hoping that their combined efforts will preserve a significant portion of the historic Cooper River watershed.

While the modern world may declare places such as Medway "unnecessary and therefore obsolete," as Charleston writer Herbert Ravenel Sass lamented in the 1930s, the easements testify to Medway's legacy for the future. Not only do they articulate the significance of Medway to those who have come before—the Smiths, the Hyrnes, the Stoneys, the Gourdines and the Legendres, to name a few—they also verify its importance for those coming after. In a world in which humans are becoming increasingly alienated from nature, a place of such ancient and ethereal loveliness, shaped by nature's powerful forces and by people with vision, can serve as both an anchor and a transforming force in the lives of its owners, its workers and its many visitors. Its story is one of change and endurance, deeply rooted in the swamps, forests and clay soils that lie along the shores of Back River. Gertrude's wish is that Medway will continue to provide a link between the land and human aspirations. Thanks to her foresight, that wish will be a reality.

ACKNOWLEDGEMENTS

I am among the countless visitors to Medway for whom Gertrude Legendre has provided inspiration and encouragement; I wish to thank her for her faith in this project and her faith in me. Her grandchildren Wendy Wood and Sandy Wood, and Sandy's wife, Sally, also contributed immeasurably to the book, beginning with its inception in 1995. Grandson Pierre Manigault was another helpful guide.

Without the meticulous and thorough research of Agnes Baldwin, Dick Côté, and archaeologist Carl Steen, we would know much less of Medway's early history. I also wish to thank Jonathan Poston, Tom Savage, Dale Rosengarten, Martha Zierden, Elise Pinckney, Leland Ferguson, Charles Kovacik, David Moltke-Hansen, and Lucy Wayne for generously sharing their scholarly expertise with me.

Former director Alex Moore and his staff at the South Carolina Historical Society, including Steve Hoffius and Peter Wilkerson, patiently shepherded me through their archives, as did Catherine Sadler, Patricia Bennett, and the rest of the staff at the Charleston Library Society, Libba Taylor at the Charleston County Library, Mark Butler of the Berkeley Museum, and Ann Bruce and Juanita Whidden at Tall Timbers Research Station.

Writers Anne Freeman, John Tibbetts, Jane Lareau, Anne Rhett, Elizabeth Hamilton, Billy Baldwin, Ted Phillips, and Edward Ball shared their knowledge, along with painter Tony Henneberg, a fellow bird watcher. The world of hunting was revealed to me by Charles Waring, Edward Lowndes, Frank Ford, Elliott Hutson, and Tony Martin.

Harriet McDougal, Serena Leonhardt, Stoney Simons, and Peter McGee introduced me to the Stoney family with a font of intriguing stories and memorabilia. Likewise, Nancy Smythe and her mother, May Conner, helped illuminate days gone by at Pine Grove and at Medway, as did Henry Lowndes, Sr., Henry Smythe, Sr., and John Bennett, Jr.

Gertie's many friends, including Wee McIver, Doogie Boocock and her daughter Leslie Barclay, Marie Snowden, Carola Kittredge, Mary Douglas, Ho Kelland, and Pat Robinson clued me in to Medway's social life, past and present.

Medway's generous and knowledgeable staff graciously welcomed me behind the scenes no matter how impromptu or inconvenient my interruption might be. I wish to thank them all, including Robert Hortman and his wife, Janet, Doris Walters, Erika Groover, Sam Washington, Sirus Washington, Robert Walbaum, Christine Lofton, Harry Wilson, Michael Kennedy, Bertha Mae Smalls, Kutana Moore, Jacqueline King, Ronald Russell, Leo Ramsey, Wanda McFann, Diane Phillips, Cynthia McKnight, Barbara Baylock, Carolyn Mack, and Mary Jefferson. Retired staff members Willie Washington, Elizabeth Gourdine, Candace Beaton, and Alva Johansson kindly shared their rememberances as well.

Connie and Pete Wyrick of Wyrick and Company are a great publishing team and the most generous of friends. Their able staff members–Charles Cornwell, Michael Robertson, Kay Wise, Simons Young, and Anne Hanahan–and designer Sally Heineman were invaluable to the project. My thanks also go to my good friends Lynn and Tom Blagden, who together with Gertie, expressed their confidence in me.

Finally, I must thank my family–my parents, Virginia and Andrew Christian, and brothers, Andy and Scott Christian, for their thoughtful comments on the manuscript; my brother-in-law, John Beach; my children Nellie and Francis, and their caretaker, Patrice Prioleau; and my husband, friend and unerring adviser, Dana Beach, who introduced me to the Lowcountry and to whom I shall always be indebted.

PHOTOGRAPHER'S NOTES

Years ago when Gertrude Legendre first spoke to me regarding photographing Medway, she knew she wanted to do a book about the plantation. She was committed to the importance of photographically expressing a sense of place at a unique moment in her lifetime. Medway *is* Gertrude Legendre, but Gertrude Legendre is also Medway, and, thus seeks always to see it differently, recognizing the land's deeper spirit through the perceptions of others. I am forever grateful to Gertie, not only for the privilege of photographing Medway and sharing those images herein, but more importantly, for her friendship, enthusiasm, and encouragement in all my endeavors since first arriving in the Lowcountry as a young man.

My special thanks extend to Robert Hortman, manager of Medway Plantation, and his wife Janet. As an accomplished wildlife carver and painter, as well as a biologist, Robert's keen observations and assistance were invaluable. He is a gifted steward of Medway and the natural kingdom therein.

It is impossible for me to think of Medway without remembering Bill Baldwin, a highly respected biologist and land consultant who managed Medway when I first arrived there 20 years ago. Bill's friendship and keen interest in my work helped direct and shape my devotion to the Lowcountry. His presence still carries on in my photography and all who care about the land. My gratitude also goes to Tony Henneberg, extremely talented artist-in-residence at Medway, for directing me to worthy subjects and places. Thanks also to Ronald Russell at Medway. All of these people are my secondary eyes and make my job much easier.

This book has been an exceptional opportunity to work in partnership with a team, all of whom are good friends and share great affection for the subject. As author of *Medway,* Virginia Beach brings depth to the book, transcending what might have been a pictorial celebration to create a compelling account of history, values, and stewardship. Sandy and Wendy Wood, Mrs. Legendre's grandchildren, helped shape the book through its formative conceptual stages. Publishers Pete and Connie Wyrick have guided us through the increasingly complicated process of developing the book. My deep gratitude goes to the Legendre family, Virginia Beach, and the Wyricks for the chance to contribute to the creative process that led to the realization of *Medway.* It was always more than an assignment; now, it is part of me, too.

BIBLIOGRAPHY

Allen, Hervey. "Back River: Medway Plantation." In *Carolina Chansons: Legends of the Lowcountry*, by DuBose Heyward and Hervey Allen. 1922. Reissue, New York: The Macmillan Company, 1924.

Baldwin, William, Jr. *Plantations of the Low Country*. Researched by Agnes Leland Baldwin. Greensboro, N.C.: Legacy Publications, 1985.

Beach, Dana, and Virginia Beach. "Lands of Great Richness." *South Carolina Wildlife*, January-February 1992, 4-13.

Beach, Virginia. "An Up & Coming Forest." *South Carolina Wildlife*, January-February 1993, 44-49.

Bennett, John. *The Treasure of Peyre Gaillard*. New York: The Century Company, 1906.

———. Papers. Letters and photographs. South Carolina Historical Society, Charleston, S.C.

Boyle, Christopher C. "Bargainers: South Carolina's Colonial Fur Traders." *Carolina Coast*, March-April 1997, 9-11.

Chaplin, Joyce E. "Tidal Rice Cultivation and the Problem of Slavery in South Carolina and Georgia, 1760-1815." *William and Mary Quarterly*, 3d. ser., 49 (1992): 29-61.

Côté, Richard N. "Medway Plantation, Back River: An Historical Outline, 1684-1993." Researched by Agnes Leland Baldwin. Prepared for Gertrude S. Legendre, Goose Creek, S.C., July 1993.

———. "Preserving the Legacy: Medway Plantation on Back River." Researched by Agnes Leland Baldwin. Prepared for Gertrude S. Legendre, Goose Creek, S.C., 1993.

Derieux, James C. "The Renaissance of the Plantation." *Country Life*, January 1932.

Elliott, William. *Carolina Sports by Land and Water: Including Incidents of Devil-Fishing, Wild-Cat, Deer & Bear Hunting, Etc.* 1846. Reprint, with an introduction by Theodore Rosengarten. Columbia, S.C.: University of South Carolina Press, 1994.

Heyward, DuBose. Foreword to *Carolina Gardens*, by E.T.H. Shaffer. New York: Huntington Press, 1937.

Irving, John B. *A Day on Cooper River*. 1842. Enlarged and edited by Louisa C. Stoney, 1932. Reprint, with notes by Samuel Gaillard Stoney, Columbia, S.C.: R.L. Bryan Company, 1969.

Kittredge, Carola. "Charleston's Grandest Dame." *Town and Country*, April 1995.

Komarek, E.V. "The Role of the Hunting Plantation in the Development of Game, Fire Ecology and Management." In *Tall Timbers Ecology and Management Conference,* Proceedings Number 16. Tallahassee: Tall Timbers Research Station, 1982.

Lane, Mills. *Architecture of the Old South: South Carolina.* Savannah: Beehive Press, 1984.

Leffingwell, William Bruce. "The Happy Hunting Grounds, also Fishing in the South." Chicago: Donohue and Henneberry, 1895. Quoted in Stuart A. Marks, *Southern Hunting in Black and White: Nature, History, and Rituals in a Carolina Community* (Princeton: Princeton University Press, 1991), 48.

Legendre, Gertrude Sanford. *The Time of My Life.* Charleston, S.C.: Wyrick and Company, 1987.

Legendre, Sidney J. "Diary Of Life At Medway Plantation: Mt. Holly, South Carolina, Beginning The Month Of May 1937." Medway Plantation Archives, Goose Creek, S.C.

Littlefield, Daniel C. *Rice and the Making of South Carolina: an Introductory Essay.* Columbia, S.C.: South Carolina Department of Archives and History, 1995.

Marks, Stuart A. *Southern Hunting in Black and White: Nature, History, and Rituals in a Carolina Community.* Princeton: Princeton University Press, 1991.

Medway Game Book 1934-1958. Medway Plantation Archives, Goose Creek, S.C.

Medway Guest Books 1930-1965, 1965-1990, 1990-present. Medway Plantation Archives, Goose Creek, S.C.

Merrens, H. Roy, ed. *The Colonial South Carolina Scene: Contemporary Views 1697-1774.* Columbia, S.C.: University of South Carolina Press, 1977.

Norris, Ann Shreve. *Pimlico Plantation: Now and Long Ago.* Mt. Pleasant, S.C.: by author, 1994.

Porcher, Richard D. *A Field Guide to the Bluff Plantation.* New Orleans, La.: The Kathleen O'Brien Foundation, 1985.

Rutledge, Archibald. "The Deer of the Southern Woods: Practical Advice on the Art of Hunting Whitetails in the Southern Pine Brush." *Field and Stream,* February 1915, 1047.

———. Papers. Letters. South Carolina Historical Society, Charleston, S.C.

Salley, A.S. "The House at Medway." *The South Carolina Historical Magazine* 33, no. 3 (July 1932): 245-246.

Saunders, Boyd, and Ann McAden. *Alfred Hutty and the Charleston Renaissance.* Orangeburg, S.C.: Sandlapper Publishing Company, 1990.

Schmidt, Albert J. "Applying Old World Habits to the New: Life in South Carolina at the Turn of the Eighteenth Century." *Huntington Library Quarterly* 25 (November 1961): 51-59.

———. "Hyrne Family Letters." *The South Carolina Historical Magazine* 63, no.3 (July 1962): 150-157.

Shaffer, E.T.H. *Carolina Gardens*. New York: Huntington Press, 1937.

Smythe, Augustine T., et al. *The Carolina Low-Country*. New York: The Macmillan Company, 1931.

Smythe-Stoney-Adger Collection. Account books, journals, letters, papers and photographs. South Carolina Historical Society, Charleston, S.C.

Snowden, Yates. *Two Scholarly Friends: Yates Snowden-John Bennett Correspondence, 1902-1932*. Edited by Mary Crow. Columbia, S.C.: University of South Carolina Press, 1993.

Steen, Carl. "Historical Archaeology at Medway Plantation, Goose Creek, S.C." Prepared for Medway Environmental Trust, Goose Creek, S.C., October 1996.

–––. "A Preliminary Report on the 1992 Excavations at Pine Grove Plantation: Berkeley County, S.C." Prepared for Historic Charleston Foundation, Charleston, S.C., 1992.

Stockton, Robert P. "Historic Resources of Berkeley County South Carolina." Charleston, S.C.: Preservation Consultants, Inc., 1990.

–––. "Plantation House Poses a Mystery." *Charleston (SC) News and Courier,* 23 November 1981.

Stoney, Samuel Gaillard. *Plantations of the Carolina Low Country*. Edited by Albert Simons and Samuel Lapham. Charleston, S.C.: Carolina Art Association, 1938.

Stoney, Samuel Gaillard, and Henry P. Staats. "Comments on Old Charleston Brickwork." Charleston, S.C., n.d.

Stoney Family. Medway Plantation Day Book, 1852. Smythe-Stoney-Adger Collection. South Carolina Historical Society, Charleston, S.C.

–––. Medway Plantation Day Book, 1872. Smythe-Stoney-Adger Collection. South Carolina Historical Society, Charleston, S.C.

–––. Medway Plantation Hunt Book, 1875-1918. Smythe-Stoney-Adger Collection. South Carolina Historical Society, Charleston, S.C.

"Up the Ashley and Cooper." *Harper's New Monthly Magazine,* December 1875, 1-24.

Wayne, Lucy B. "Burning Brick: A Study of a Lowcountry Industry." Ph.D. diss., University of Florida, 1992.

Weir, Robert M. *Colonial South Carolina: A History.* Millwood, N.Y.: KTO Press, 1983.

INDEX

Published by Wyrick & Company
P.O. Box 89
Charleston, S.C. 29402

Copyright © 1999 by Medway Environmental Trust
Photographs copyright © 1999 by Thomas Blagden, Jr.
All rights reserved.

Designed by Sally Heineman.
Printed in Hong Kong.

Library of Congress Cataloging-in-Publication Data

Beach, Virginia.
Medway / Virginia Christian Beach;
principal photography by Thomas Blagden, Jr.
p. cm.
Includes bibliographical references (p.119) and index.
ISBN 0-941711-38-2
1. Medway (S.C.)--History. 2. Medway (S.C.)--Pictorial works.
3. Plantation life--South Carolina--Berkeley County.
4. Legendre, Gertrude Sanford, 1902-   .
5. Legendre, Getrude Sanford, 1902-   --Family. I. Title.
F279.M37B4   1999
975.7'93--dc21   99-10585
CIP

Contents page illustration by Robert Hortman.
Photograph credits: Courtesy of John Bennett, pages 27, 28, 31;
Thomas Blagden, Jr., pages 5, 48-49, 65-74, 76-77, 88-89, 98-99,
101, 102, 108-109, 112; Toni Frissell, pages 40, 57, 86, 91, 97;
Mick Hales (courtesy *Veranda*), pages viii-1, 33, 47 (bottom), 50,
56, 58; South Carolina Historical Society, page 15;
Wade Spees, page 61; Herbert Watkins, page vi-vii, 34-35, 43.
All other photographs are from the Medway archives.